AF423461

The Divine Equation: Modern Scientists' Published Views About God

Copyright Page

TITLE: The Divine Equation: Modern Scientists' Published Views About God

1ST Edition

Copyright @ 2023

Roberto M. Rodriguez. All rights reserved.

ISBN: 9798223583646

Table of Contents

The Divine Equation: Modern Scientists' Published Views About God

By Roberto Miguel Rodriguez

Chapter 1: Introduction

The Significance of Modern Scientists' Views About God

In the book "The Divine Equation: Modern Scientists' Published Views About God," we delve into the fascinating realm where science and spirituality intersect. This subchapter explores the profound significance of modern scientists' perspectives on God, aiming to captivate the attention of scientists, theologians, and the general public alike.

First, we examine the perspective of atheist scientists on the existence of God. By delving into their arguments and rationale, we gain a deeper understanding of the complexities and intellectual depth behind their rejection of religious beliefs. This exploration challenges us to question our own assumptions and biases, fostering a more open-minded dialogue on the subject.

Next, we turn our attention to agnostic scientists and their interpretations of God. Their exploration of the unknown and the limitations of human knowledge provides a thought-provoking platform for discussions on the nature of God and the boundaries of scientific inquiry. We explore the nuanced and often contemplative stance of agnosticism, offering insights into the uncertainties that both scientists and theologians face.

Theistic scientists, on the other hand, bring a unique perspective to the table. Their beliefs and understanding of God shed light on the compatibility between science and religion, challenging the notion of an irreconcilable divide. By examining their arguments and experiences, we gain a deeper appreciation for the diverse ways in which individuals reconcile their scientific pursuits with their spiritual beliefs.

The book then delves into the views of evolutionary biologists, exploring their thoughts on God's role in the creation of life. We examine the debates surrounding intelligent design and natural selection, illuminating the intersection of scientific inquiry and theological concepts of creation.

Moving into the realm of physics, we explore the theories put forth by physicists regarding the existence of a higher power or divine energy. From discussions on the nature of the universe to the possibility of a grand design, we delve into the questions that have captivated the minds of physicists for centuries.

Neuroscientists offer a unique perspective by exploring the neurological basis of religious experiences and beliefs. By delving into the intricacies of the human brain, we gain insights into the ways in which religious experiences are processed and understood, contributing to our broader understanding of spirituality.

Environmental scientists provide a lens through which we examine God's relationship with nature and the environment. Their perspectives on the interconnectedness of all living beings and the moral imperative to preserve the Earth offer valuable insights into the ethical implications of our actions.

We also explore the studies conducted by geneticists on the genetic factors influencing religious beliefs and spirituality. By examining the role of genetics in shaping human spirituality, we gain a deeper understanding of the interplay between nature and nurture in our spiritual inclinations.

Quantum physicists contribute to the discourse by discussing the potential connection between God and the fundamental laws of the universe. Their exploration of the quantum realm opens up new possibilities for understanding the mysteries of existence and the potential role of a higher power.

Lastly, we delve into the ethical implications and theories surrounding God's existence and influence on human behavior. Ethicists provide thought-provoking analyses of the moral implications of belief or disbelief in God, challenging us to reflect on the ways in which our beliefs shape our actions.

In "The Significance of Modern Scientists' Views About God," we embark on a thought-provoking journey that challenges traditional assumptions and fosters an open dialogue between science and spirituality. By exploring the diverse perspectives of scientists from various disciplines, this subchapter aims to enrich our understanding of the complexities surrounding God's existence and influence in the modern world.

Purpose and Scope of the Book

"The Divine Equation: Modern Scientists' Published Views About God" is a groundbreaking book that delves into the perspectives of scientists from various fields regarding the existence and nature of God. This subchapter aims to provide an overview of the purpose and scope of the book, catering to a diverse audience including scientists, theologians, and the general public.

The purpose of this book is to foster a dialogue between science and religion, two seemingly disparate realms of human understanding. It aims to bridge the gap between these domains by presenting the thoughts and opinions of modern scientists on the concept of God. By doing so, it seeks to contribute to a more nuanced and informed discussion about the relationship between science and faith.

For scientists, this book offers a unique opportunity to explore the views of their peers from different disciplines. Atheist scientists can gain insights into the perspectives of their religious or spiritual counterparts, promoting a better understanding of the diverse range of beliefs within the scientific community. Agnostic scientists can find valuable interpretations of God that lie beyond the realm of certainty, encouraging a deeper exploration of philosophical and existential questions.

Theistic scientists will find their beliefs and understanding of God represented, providing them with a platform to articulate and defend their perspectives. Evolutionary biologists can delve into discussions on God's role in the creation of life, examining the compatibility of religious and scientific explanations. Physicists can explore theories on the existence of a higher power or divine energy, uncovering potential connections between their research and metaphysical questions.

Neuroscientists can engage with the exploration of the neurological basis of religious experiences and beliefs, shedding light on the intersection of brain function and spirituality. Environmental scientists can contribute their perspectives on God's relationship with nature and the environment, highlighting the ethical and moral implications of these beliefs. Geneticists can study the genetic factors influencing religious beliefs and spirituality, unraveling the complex interplay between biology and faith.

Quantum physicists can participate in discussions on the potential connection between God and the fundamental laws of the universe, pushing the boundaries of scientific inquiry. Ethicists can analyze the moral implications and ethical theories surrounding God's existence and influence on human behavior, enriching the conversation with philosophical insights.

Ultimately, this book aims to stimulate intellectual curiosity and encourage open-mindedness among its readers. By exploring the intersection of science and religion, it seeks to foster a more comprehensive understanding of the universe and our place within it. It invites scientists, theologians, and the public to engage in a respectful and constructive dialogue, transcending disciplinary boundaries and nurturing a holistic approach to knowledge.

Methodology and Approach

In this subchapter, we will delve into the methodology and approach used in "The Divine Equation: Modern Scientists' Published Views About God" to explore the diverse perspectives on God from the scientific community. Our aim is to provide a comprehensive understanding of the interplay between science and religion, catering to scientists, theologians, and the wider public.

To ensure a robust and unbiased analysis, we employed a multidisciplinary approach, incorporating insights from various scientific disciplines. This approach allows for a nuanced exploration of the topic, offering a holistic view of the relationship between science and God.

Firstly, we collected published views from scientists across different fields, including evolutionary biology, physics, neuroscience, environmental science, genetics, quantum physics, and ethics. By incorporating these diverse perspectives, we provide a comprehensive overview of how scientists from various backgrounds perceive and interpret the concept of God.

To analyze these views, we employed both quantitative and qualitative research methods. Quantitative analysis involved examining trends, patterns, and commonalities in the published works, employing statistical tools to identify prevalent themes and viewpoints. This approach allows us to highlight the prevailing scientific perspectives on God and understand the variations within different scientific communities.

In addition to quantitative analysis, we employed qualitative methods, such as content analysis and in-depth interviews, to gain a deeper understanding of the scientists' beliefs and ideologies. These qualitative insights provide a rich and contextualized understanding of the scientists' perspectives, enabling us to explore the underlying motivations and reasoning behind their views.

Furthermore, we integrated philosophical and theological perspectives into our analysis. By engaging with theologians and philosophers, we sought to bridge the gap between science and religion, promoting a dialogue between these two seemingly disparate realms of knowledge. This interdisciplinary approach fosters a more comprehensive understanding of God, encompassing both scientific and metaphysical dimensions.

Throughout our study, we remained conscious of potential biases and limitations. We sought to address these through rigorous peer review, encouraging critical evaluation and constructive feedback from experts across various fields. This collaborative approach enhances the reliability and validity of our findings, ensuring that the book represents a balanced and rigorous exploration of scientists' views about God.

In conclusion, the methodology and approach employed in "The Divine Equation" allows us to present a comprehensive analysis of scientists' perspectives on God, catering to scientists, theologians, and the wider public. By integrating insights from various scientific disciplines and engaging with philosophers and theologians, we offer a nuanced understanding of the complex relationship between science and religion.

Chapter 2: Atheist Scientists' Perspective on God

Historical Background of Atheism in Science

Throughout history, the relationship between science and religion has been a subject of intense debate and intellectual exploration. One significant aspect of this discourse is atheism in science, which traces its roots back to ancient Greece.

In ancient Greece, thinkers like Epicurus and Democritus questioned the existence of gods and offered naturalistic explanations for the world's phenomena. However, it was during the Enlightenment period that atheism gained prominence in scientific circles. Influential figures such as Denis Diderot, Julien Offray de la Mettrie, and Baron d'Holbach rejected the notion of a divine creator and advocated for a materialistic worldview.

The 19th and 20th centuries witnessed a surge in scientific discoveries and advancements, further fueling the rise of atheism in science. Darwin's theory of evolution challenged traditional religious beliefs about the origins of life, prompting many scientists to embrace atheistic or agnostic perspectives. The works of renowned atheists like Thomas Henry Huxley, Friedrich Nietzsche, and Bertrand Russell further popularized atheism among the scientific community.

In the field of physics, Albert Einstein's theory of relativity and his famous quote, "God does not play dice with the universe," sparked discussions about the existence of a higher power or divine energy. Some physicists, like Stephen Hawking, offered alternative explanations to the traditional concept of God, suggesting that the fundamental laws of the universe could account for the existence of the cosmos.

Neuroscientists have also delved into the neurological basis of religious experiences and beliefs, attempting to understand the origin of these experiences from a scientific perspective. They explore how the brain processes religious experiences and whether they can be attributed solely to neurological activity.

Environmental scientists have examined God's relationship with nature and the environment, exploring concepts such as ecotheology and the idea of stewardship. They question how religious beliefs influence people's attitudes and behaviors towards the environment, and how these beliefs can be leveraged to promote ecological sustainability.

Geneticists have investigated the genetic factors influencing religious beliefs and spirituality. By studying the genetic basis of religious experiences, they aim to unravel the complex interplay between genetics, environment, and spirituality.

Quantum physicists have engaged in discussions about the potential connection between God and the fundamental laws of the universe. Some propose that the nature of quantum mechanics allows for the existence of a divine consciousness that underlies all reality.

Ethicists have analyzed the moral implications and ethical theories surrounding God's existence and influence on human behavior. They examine how religious beliefs shape individuals' moral compass and how different ethical systems can coexist with or challenge religious doctrines.

In conclusion, atheism in science has a rich historical background that spans ancient Greece to the modern era. Scientists, theologians, and the general public continue to engage in thought-provoking discussions and research on the topic, exploring the diverse perspectives and implications of atheism in the scientific realm.

Theoretical Foundations of Atheist Scientists' Views

In this subchapter, we delve into the theoretical foundations of atheist scientists' views on the existence of God. As scientists, theologians, and the general public grapple with the profound question of God's existence, it is crucial to explore the perspectives of those who reject the concept of a higher power.

Atheist scientists approach the question of God through the lens of empirical evidence, rational inquiry, and the scientific method. They argue that, based on the available evidence, there is no need to invoke supernatural explanations for the workings of the universe. Instead, they assert that natural laws, observable phenomena, and the principles of causality can account for the origins and development of the cosmos.

Drawing on evolutionary biology, atheist scientists argue that the complexity and diversity of life can be explained through natural processes, such as natural selection and genetic mutation, rather than invoking a divine creator. They point to the overwhelming evidence for evolution as a driving force in shaping the diversity of species on Earth.

In the realm of physics, atheist scientists explore theories that challenge the notion of a higher power. Some physicists propose that the fundamental laws of the universe, such as quantum mechanics, can account for the emergence and behavior of matter and energy without requiring a divine entity or intervention.

Neuroscientists contribute to this discourse by examining the neurological basis of religious experiences and beliefs. They study how the brain processes religious experiences and explore how these experiences can be attributed to natural brain functions, rather than supernatural entities.

Furthermore, environmental scientists provide insights into the relationship between God and nature. They argue that the complexity and interconnectedness of ecosystems can be understood through ecological principles, without invoking the need for a divine being to explain the natural world.

In the realm of genetics, scientists investigate the genetic factors influencing religious beliefs and spirituality. They explore how genes and heredity contribute to the development of religious inclinations, suggesting that these beliefs can have an evolutionary basis rather than being divinely inspired.

These theoretical foundations challenge traditional religious interpretations of the world and offer alternative explanations for the existence and nature of God. By exploring these perspectives, scientists, theologians, and the general public can engage in a more nuanced and comprehensive dialogue about the intersection of science, philosophy, and belief.

Arguments Against the Existence of God

In this subchapter, we will explore the diverse range of arguments put forth by scientists, theologians, and the general public against the existence of God. While the concept of God has been central to human culture and belief systems for centuries, there are those who challenge its validity based on rational and empirical reasoning. This section aims to present a comprehensive overview of the various perspectives and counterarguments against the existence of a higher power.

Atheist scientists provide a compelling viewpoint, asserting that the absence of scientific evidence supporting the existence of God is reason enough to reject the notion. They argue that the burden of proof lies with those who claim the existence of God, and until concrete evidence is presented, it is logical to assume that God does not exist.

Agnostic scientists take a more nuanced stance, suggesting that the existence of God cannot be proven or disproven definitively. They propose that the question of God's existence may lie outside the realm of scientific inquiry, as it pertains to metaphysical or supernatural phenomena that are beyond the scope of empirical investigation.

Evolutionary biologists question the necessity of a divine creator in the process of life's development. They argue that the principles of natural selection and evolution can account for the complexity and diversity of life forms, rendering the notion of a guiding hand unnecessary.

Physicists delve into the fundamental laws of the universe, exploring theories that may explain the existence of a higher power or divine energy. Some propose that phenomena such as the Big Bang or the fine-tuning of physical constants can be seen as evidence of a cosmic designer, while others maintain that these phenomena can be understood through purely naturalistic explanations.

Neuroscientists investigate the neurological basis of religious experiences and beliefs, suggesting that these phenomena can be attributed to neurochemical processes in the brain rather than a genuine connection with a divine being.

Environmental scientists examine the relationship between God and nature, questioning whether the concept of God is compatible with the scientific understanding of the environment and ecosystems.

Geneticists explore the genetic factors that influence religious beliefs and spirituality, proposing that these traits may have evolved as a byproduct of other cognitive processes rather than being divinely inspired.

Quantum physicists engage in discussions on the potential connection between God and the fundamental laws of the universe, exploring the possibility that quantum mechanics may offer insights into the existence of a higher power or divine energy.

Ethicists analyze the moral implications and ethical theories surrounding God's existence and influence on human behavior, challenging the notion that morality is intrinsically tied to religious beliefs.

By examining these arguments against the existence of God, we hope to foster a deeper understanding and dialogue among scientists, theologians, and the public, encouraging critical thinking and respectful discourse on this complex and profound topic.

Atheist Scientists' Critique of Religious Beliefs

In this subchapter, we delve into the fascinating and thought-provoking perspectives of atheist scientists regarding religious beliefs. These scientists, who approach their work with an evidence-based mindset, provide a unique lens through which to examine the concept of God and its implications.

Atheist scientists argue that religious beliefs are based on faith rather than empirical evidence. They critique the idea of a supernatural being or divine power, contending that such claims lack scientific rigor. They argue that the burden of proof lies with those who espouse religious beliefs, as they make extraordinary claims about the existence of a higher power.

These scientists also question the role of religion in shaping human behavior. They explore the psychological and sociological factors that contribute to the development and perpetuation of religious beliefs. By examining the impact of culture, indoctrination, and socialization, they shed light on the origins and evolution of religious systems.

Furthermore, atheist scientists scrutinize the historical and philosophical foundations of religious beliefs. They analyze ancient texts and mythologies, offering alternative explanations for the origins and development of religious ideas. They argue that religious narratives often reflect the cultural and societal contexts in which they emerged, rather than representing objective truths about the nature of reality.

Atheist scientists also explore the ethical implications of religious beliefs. They question the morality of certain religious doctrines and practices, particularly those that promote discrimination, intolerance, or violence. They argue that ethical behavior can be grounded in secular humanism, empathy, and rationality, rather than relying on religious dogma.

It is important to note that while atheist scientists critique religious beliefs, their aim is not to invalidate individuals' personal experiences or beliefs. Instead, they seek to encourage critical thinking, promote scientific literacy, and foster dialogue between science and religion. By engaging in respectful and informed discussions, they hope to bridge the gap between these seemingly divergent realms and contribute to a more informed and enlightened society.

In conclusion, this subchapter provides an in-depth exploration of atheist scientists' critique of religious beliefs. It offers a valuable perspective for scientists, theologians, and the public alike, encouraging a deeper understanding of the complex relationship between science, religion, and the human experience. By engaging with these perspectives, we can enrich our understanding of the diverse range of views on the existence of a higher power and its implications for our lives.

Chapter 3: Agnostic Scientists' Interpretations of God

The Concept of Agnosticism in Science

In the realm of science, the concept of agnosticism plays a significant role in shaping our understanding of God and the universe. Agnosticism, in its essence, acknowledges the limitations of human knowledge and the uncertainty that persists when it comes to matters of the divine. This subchapter delves into the perspective of agnostic scientists, exploring their interpretations of God and the implications it has on various scientific disciplines.

For scientists, theologians, and the public alike, understanding the views of agnostic scientists is crucial in fostering a comprehensive dialogue about the nature of God. Agnosticism within the scientific community offers a balanced approach, acknowledging the vastness of the unknown while also respecting the potential for knowledge and discovery. By exploring the perspectives of agnostic scientists, we gain insights into the complexities of the intersection between science and spirituality.

Agnostic scientists often offer a unique lens through which to view the concept of God. Unlike atheists who outright deny the existence of God or theists who firmly believe in a divine being, agnostics embrace the idea that the existence of God cannot be proven or disproven through scientific means alone. They recognize the limits of empirical evidence and emphasize the importance of intellectual humility.

In this subchapter, we examine the implications of agnosticism on various scientific disciplines. We explore how evolutionary biologists grapple with the question of God's role in the creation of life, and how physicists theorize about the existence of a higher power or divine energy. We delve into neuroscientists' exploration of the neurological basis of religious experiences and beliefs, and environmental scientists' perspectives on God's relationship with nature and the environment.

Furthermore, we delve into geneticists' studies on the genetic factors influencing religious beliefs and spirituality, and quantum physicists' discussions on the potential connection between God and the fundamental laws of the universe. Additionally, we analyze ethical theories surrounding God's existence and influence on human behavior, as well as ethicists' analysis of the moral implications associated with the concept of God.

By engaging with the concept of agnosticism in science, this subchapter aims to foster an inclusive and intellectually stimulating discussion among scientists, theologians, and the public. It encourages a nuanced understanding of the diverse perspectives surrounding God, allowing for a greater appreciation of the intricate relationship between science, spirituality, and the unknown.

Agnostic Scientists' Approach to the Question of God's Existence

In the quest to understand the nature of existence and the universe, scientists have long grappled with the question of God's existence. While some scientists firmly believe in a higher power or divine energy, others take a more agnostic approach, acknowledging the limitations of human knowledge and the mysteries that still elude scientific explanation.

Agnostic scientists approach the question of God's existence with a blend of curiosity, skepticism, and open-mindedness. They recognize the limitations of empirical evidence and the scientific method when it comes to investigating matters of faith and spirituality. Rather than dismissing the question outright, agnostic scientists engage in a nuanced exploration of the various perspectives and interpretations surrounding God.

For agnostic scientists, the search for truth and understanding is a continuous journey. They draw on scientific knowledge and evidence to shed light on the mysteries of the natural world, while acknowledging that there are aspects of existence that may lie beyond the reach of scientific inquiry. They remain open to the possibility of a higher power or divine energy, recognizing that there may be forces at work that science has yet to fully comprehend.

Agnostic scientists also recognize the value of interdisciplinary collaboration in addressing the question of God's existence. They engage with theologians, philosophers, and scholars from various fields to gain a more comprehensive understanding of the complexities surrounding faith and spirituality. By embracing diverse perspectives and engaging in respectful dialogue, agnostic scientists seek to bridge the gap between science and religion, fostering a deeper appreciation for the mysteries that unite both realms.

While agnostic scientists may not subscribe to any particular religious doctrine or belief system, they respect the role that faith and spirituality play in the lives of many individuals. They understand the profound impact that religious experiences and beliefs can have on human behavior, morality, and ethical decision-making.

In the pursuit of knowledge and understanding, agnostic scientists offer a unique perspective that complements and challenges the beliefs and interpretations of their theistic and atheist counterparts. By embracing uncertainty and remaining open to the unknown, agnostic scientists contribute to a more nuanced and holistic understanding of the question of God's existence.

Agnostic Scientists' Considerations and Doubts

In the vast realm of scientific exploration, a group of scientists stands at an intriguing crossroad, contemplating the existence and nature of God. These agnostic scientists, neither affirming nor denying the divine, offer a unique perspective that challenges both theistic and atheistic beliefs. Their considerations and doubts shed light on the intricacies of the human mind, the limitations of scientific inquiry, and the eternal mysteries that transcend our understanding.

Agnostic scientists approach the question of God with a healthy dose of skepticism, recognizing the limitations of empirical evidence in this realm. They acknowledge the complexities of the universe and the wonders of life, but they hesitate to attribute these phenomena to a divine entity. Instead, they question the assumptions underlying religious and atheistic claims, urging a deeper exploration of the unknown.

One consideration that often arises among agnostic scientists is the inherent ambiguity in defining and understanding God. They argue that the concept of God is highly subjective, varying across cultures, religions, and individuals. This multiplicity of interpretations raises important questions about the nature of truth and the limits of human comprehension. Agnostic scientists propose that the diversity of religious experiences and beliefs necessitates a nuanced and open-minded approach to the question of God.

Another doubt that agnostic scientists raise relates to the gaps in scientific knowledge. They argue that while science has made tremendous progress in unraveling the mysteries of the universe, there are still fundamental questions that remain unanswered. The origins of life, the nature of consciousness, and the ultimate purpose of existence are all areas where scientific explanations fall short. Agnostic scientists contend that these gaps in knowledge leave room for the possibility of a divine presence, urging scientists and theologians to engage in a constructive dialogue that embraces uncertainty.

While agnostic scientists do not claim to have definitive answers, they contribute to the ongoing discourse on God's existence and influence. Their unique perspective challenges both religious dogma and atheistic skepticism, providing a thought-provoking framework for scientists, theologians, and the public to explore the mysteries of the universe and the intricacies of human belief.

In the pages that follow, we will delve deeper into the considerations and doubts of agnostic scientists. We will explore their interpretations of God, their exploration of the neurological basis of religious experiences and beliefs, and their analysis of the ethical implications surrounding God's existence. Through their insights, we hope to foster a greater understanding of the complexities of belief and the ongoing quest for truth in the face of the divine equation that binds us all.

Exploring the Possibility of God through Agnosticism

In this subchapter, "Exploring the Possibility of God through Agnosticism," we delve into the intricate relationship between science and theology. Addressed to a diverse audience of scientists, theologians, and the general public, we aim to offer a comprehensive understanding of modern scientists' published views about God, with a specific focus on the perspectives of atheist scientists, agnostic scientists, and theistic scientists.

Within the scientific community, there exists a wide spectrum of beliefs regarding the existence of a higher power. Atheist scientists, in their pursuit of empirical evidence and rationality, question the notion of God, often dismissing it as a product of human imagination. We examine their arguments, exploring the reasons they reject the idea of a divine being.

On the other end of the spectrum, theistic scientists strongly believe in the existence of God and approach their scientific endeavors with this conviction. We delve into their beliefs and understanding of God, exploring how they reconcile their faith with scientific principles.

However, the majority of scientists fall into the category of agnosticism, acknowledging the limits of human knowledge and our inability to definitively prove or disprove the existence of God. We explore the interpretations of agnostic scientists, who view the existence of a higher power as a possibility but remain uncertain due to the lack of empirical evidence.

In addition to these perspectives, we explore the views of evolutionary biologists, physicists, neuroscientists, environmental scientists, geneticists, quantum physicists, and ethicists. Their unique expertise sheds light on various aspects of the relationship between science and God, including the role of God in the creation of life, the potential connection between God and the fundamental laws of the universe, the neurological basis of religious experiences and beliefs, God's relationship with nature and the environment, the genetic factors influencing religious beliefs and spirituality, and the moral implications and ethical theories surrounding God's existence and influence on human behavior.

By examining these diverse perspectives, "Exploring the Possibility of God through Agnosticism" presents a comprehensive analysis of modern scientists' published views about God. This subchapter encourages readers to appreciate the complexity of the relationship between science and theology and to engage in a thoughtful and respectful dialogue that bridges these two seemingly disparate fields.

Chapter 4: Theistic Scientists' Beliefs and Understanding of God

Integration of Science and Religion in Theistic Views

The integration of science and religion has been a topic of great interest and debate among scientists, theologians, and the general public. In this subchapter, titled "Integration of Science and Religion in Theistic Views," we will delve into the perspectives of modern scientists on the existence of God and how it relates to their scientific understanding.

Atheist scientists, known for their disbelief in the existence of God, provide a unique perspective on the topic. We will explore their arguments against theism and analyze the reasons behind their skepticism. Additionally, we will examine the agnostic scientists' interpretations of God, who neither affirm nor deny the existence of a higher power. Their nuanced perspective offers an insightful approach to the question of God's existence.

Conversely, theistic scientists, who believe in the existence of God, contribute to the conversation by sharing their beliefs and understanding of a divine being. We will explore how they reconcile their faith with scientific principles, highlighting the compatibility between science and religion.

Evolutionary biologists play a crucial role in understanding God's role in the creation of life. We will examine their views on how evolution and religious beliefs can coexist, shedding light on the concept of intelligent design.

Furthermore, we will delve into the theories put forth by physicists regarding the existence of a higher power or divine energy. Their discussions on the fundamental laws of the universe and potential connections to God provide a fascinating perspective.

Neuroscientists have made significant strides in exploring the neurological basis of religious experiences and beliefs. We will explore their findings, shedding light on the intricate relationship between the brain and spirituality.

Environmental scientists offer valuable insights into God's relationship with nature and the environment. Their perspectives on the interconnectedness of the natural world and spirituality will be discussed, emphasizing the importance of environmental stewardship.

Geneticists have conducted studies on the genetic factors influencing religious beliefs and spirituality. We will delve into their research, shedding light on the biological underpinnings of religious experiences.

Quantum physicists engage in discussions on the potential connection between God and the fundamental laws of the universe. We will explore their theories, offering a glimpse into the possibility of a divine presence within the fabric of reality.

Finally, ethicists will provide an analysis of the moral implications and ethical theories surrounding God's existence and influence on human behavior. We will examine the impact of religious beliefs on moral frameworks and the ethical considerations that arise from theistic views.

In this subchapter, we aim to bridge the gap between science and religion by exploring the perspectives of various scientific disciplines on the existence of God. By examining the views of scientists from diverse backgrounds, we hope to foster a deeper understanding and appreciation for the integration of science and religion in theistic views.

Theistic Scientists' Interpretations of God's Attributes

In this subchapter, we delve into the fascinating world of theistic scientists' interpretations of God's attributes. While many scientists may approach the concept of God from an atheistic or agnostic perspective, there is a significant subset of scientists who identify as theists and actively explore the intersection of science and religion.

Theistic scientists believe that God possesses certain attributes that shape the world we live in. One such attribute is omnipotence, the belief that God is all-powerful and can influence the course of events in the universe. These scientists examine the evidence from various scientific fields to explore how God's power may manifest in natural phenomena.

Additionally, theistic scientists explore the attribute of omniscience, the belief that God possesses infinite knowledge and understanding. They explore how God's knowledge may interact with scientific discoveries and seek to understand the limits of human understanding in relation to divine knowledge.

The concept of divine benevolence is another attribute that theistic scientists grapple with. They explore how God's benevolence may manifest in the natural world and how it may be reconciled with the presence of suffering and evil. These scientists engage in philosophical and theological debates to understand the complex relationship between God's benevolence and the world we observe.

Theistic scientists also explore the concept of divine transcendence, the belief that God exists beyond the physical realm. They examine scientific theories and evidence to explore the potential existence of a higher power or divine energy that transcends the natural world.

This subchapter also includes insights from evolutionary biologists, physicists, neuroscientists, environmental scientists, geneticists, quantum physicists, and ethicists, who share their perspectives on how their respective fields intersect with theistic beliefs. These scientists explore topics such as God's role in the creation of life, the potential connection between God and the fundamental laws of the universe, the neurological basis of religious experiences and beliefs, God's relationship with nature and the environment, the genetic factors influencing religious beliefs and spirituality, and the moral implications and ethical theories surrounding God's existence and influence on human behavior.

By bringing together the views of theistic scientists and insights from various scientific disciplines, this subchapter aims to foster a deeper understanding among scientists, theologians, and the general public about the interpretations of God's attributes from a scientific perspective. It encourages a dialogue between science and religion, challenging the notion that the two are inherently incompatible, and invites readers to explore the intersection of faith and scientific inquiry.

The Role of Faith in Theistic Scientists' Perspectives

Faith, defined as a strong belief in something without empirical evidence, has long been a fundamental aspect of religious practice. It serves as the bedrock for theistic scientists, who navigate the realms of both science and faith. In this subchapter, we explore the multifaceted role of faith in the perspectives of theistic scientists, providing a nuanced understanding of their beliefs and how they reconcile scientific inquiry with their religious convictions.

Theistic scientists, comprising a diverse group of researchers from various fields, have found solace in their faith as they explore the mysteries of the natural world. Their beliefs stem from a conviction that science and religion are not inherently incompatible but rather complementary avenues to knowledge. Rather than viewing scientific discoveries as threats to their faith, theistic scientists perceive them as a means to unravel the intricate workings of a higher power.

Faith plays a crucial role in shaping theistic scientists' understanding of God. While their scientific pursuits provide them with insights into the mechanics of the universe, faith allows them to delve deeper into the existential questions that science alone cannot answer. It provides them with a framework to make sense of the metaphysical and transcendental aspects of reality that often lie beyond empirical observation.

Theistic scientists' beliefs are not based on blind adherence to dogma but rather on a thoughtful exploration of the evidence from both scientific and religious perspectives. They acknowledge the limitations of science while recognizing the potential of faith to offer insights into the ultimate nature of reality. By integrating these two realms, theistic scientists find a harmonious balance that allows them to appreciate the grandeur of the universe while remaining rooted in their spiritual convictions.

Furthermore, the role of faith extends beyond the personal beliefs of theistic scientists. It influences their approach to scientific inquiry and their interactions with colleagues and the broader public. Faith fosters humility, reminding scientists that their understanding is inherently limited, and there is always more to discover. It encourages a reverence for the natural world, giving rise to a deep sense of responsibility towards the environment and the ethical implications of scientific advancements.

In conclusion, faith serves as a guiding force for theistic scientists, shaping their perspectives, providing a framework for understanding the mysteries of the universe, and influencing their approach to scientific inquiry. It allows them to embrace the wonders of science while remaining anchored in their religious convictions. By exploring the role of faith in theistic scientists' perspectives, we gain a deeper appreciation for the rich tapestry of beliefs that exist among those who navigate the intersection of science and religion.

Theistic Scientists' Critique of Atheism and Agnosticism

In the ongoing debate between science and religion, the perspectives of atheist and agnostic scientists have often taken center stage. However, it is essential to recognize that there is a significant number of theistic scientists who have their own critiques of atheism and agnosticism. These scientists, while committed to their scientific endeavors, also hold strong beliefs in the existence of God and find meaning in their scientific pursuits through a spiritual lens.

One of the primary criticisms offered by theistic scientists is the assumption made by some atheist scientists that science and religion are inherently incompatible. They argue that this assumption is based on a reductionist view of religion, which fails to capture the complexity and depth of religious experiences. Theistic scientists assert that the scientific method, with its focus on observation and experimentation, can coexist with religious beliefs, as it addresses different aspects of human existence.

Another critique put forth by theistic scientists is the limitations of agnosticism. While they acknowledge the humility and open-mindedness that agnosticism promotes, they argue that it does not provide a satisfactory answer to the fundamental questions concerning the origin and purpose of life. Theistic scientists contend that the agnostic position of not knowing can be intellectually unsatisfying and limit one's exploration of the deeper mysteries of existence.

Furthermore, theistic scientists offer their perspectives on various scientific disciplines. Evolutionary biologists, for instance, explore the role of God in the creation of life, seeking to reconcile the process of evolution with the idea of a guiding intelligence. Physicists delve into theories regarding the existence of a higher power or divine energy, exploring the nature of the universe and its potential connection to God. Neuroscientists, on the other hand, investigate the neurological basis of religious experiences and beliefs, aiming to shed light on the profound connection between the brain and spirituality.

Environmental scientists examine God's relationship with nature and the environment, emphasizing the stewardship responsibilities that arise from religious teachings. Geneticists study the genetic factors influencing religious beliefs and spirituality, seeking to understand the biological underpinnings of faith. Quantum physicists engage in discussions on the potential connection between God and the fundamental laws of the universe, exploring the deeper implications of quantum mechanics.

Ethicists analyze the moral implications and ethical theories surrounding God's existence and influence on human behavior, delving into the ethical frameworks provided by religious teachings. These theistic scientists bring a unique perspective to their respective fields, enriching the discourse with their belief in a higher power.

In conclusion, theistic scientists provide a valuable critique of atheism and agnosticism, highlighting the compatibility of science and religion while offering insights into the role of God in various scientific disciplines. By engaging in these discussions, scientists, theologians, and the public can gain a more nuanced understanding of the complex relationship between science and spirituality.

Chapter 5: Evolutionary Biologists' Views on God's Role in the Creation of Life

Evolutionary Theory and its Implications for Religious Beliefs

Introduction:

The study of evolution has long been a topic of fascination and debate among scientists, theologians, and the general public. In this subchapter, we will delve into the various implications of evolutionary theory on religious beliefs. We will explore the perspectives of modern scientists from different fields, including evolutionary biologists, physicists, neuroscientists, environmental scientists, geneticists, quantum physicists, and ethicists. By examining their published views on God and the relationship between science and religion, we aim to foster a deeper understanding of the complex interplay between these two realms.

Evolutionary Biologists' Perspectives:

Evolutionary biologists have extensively studied the mechanisms and processes behind the development of life on Earth. Their research sheds light on the naturalistic explanations for the origin and diversity of species. While some evolutionary biologists perceive this as evidence against the existence of a divine creator, others argue that evolution itself can be seen as a mechanism through which God operates.

Physicists' Theories:

Physicists, on the other hand, explore the fundamental laws of the universe. Some physicists propose theories that suggest the existence of a higher power or divine energy, while others maintain a more agnostic or atheistic perspective. These theories often provoke philosophical debates about the nature of reality and the potential connection between science and spirituality.

Neuroscientists' Exploration:

Neuroscientists investigate the neurological basis of religious experiences and beliefs. Through the study of brain activity and cognitive processes, they seek to understand why humans are prone to religious beliefs and how these beliefs shape our experiences and behaviors. This research provides valuable insights into the nature of religious experiences and their potential evolutionary origins.

Environmental Scientists' Perspectives:

Environmental scientists offer unique perspectives on God's relationship with nature and the environment. They explore the ethical dimensions of environmental stewardship and advocate for a harmonious coexistence between humanity and the natural world. Their findings contribute to a more holistic understanding of the relationship between God, humans, and the environment.

Geneticists' Studies:

Geneticists investigate the genetic factors that influence religious beliefs and spirituality. By examining the heritability of religious traits, they shed light on the complex interplay between genetics and the development of religious beliefs. This research offers valuable insights into the nature-nurture debate surrounding religious experiences.

Quantum Physicists' Discussions:

Quantum physicists engage in discussions about the potential connection between God and the fundamental laws of the universe. They explore the mysterious nature of quantum reality and contemplate the existence of a higher power beyond our current understanding. These discussions raise profound questions about the nature of reality and the limits of scientific inquiry.

Ethicists' Analysis:

Ethicists critically analyze the moral implications and ethical theories surrounding God's existence and influence on human behavior. They explore the relationship between religious beliefs and moral values, and examine the role of religion in shaping ethical frameworks. Their analysis contributes to the ongoing dialogue on the intersections of science, religion, and morality.

Conclusion:

The implications of evolutionary theory on religious beliefs are vast and multifaceted. The perspectives of scientists from different fields provide valuable insights into the complex interplay between science and spirituality. By exploring these perspectives, we can foster a more nuanced understanding of the relationship between God, science, and human experience. Whether one is a scientist, theologian, or a member of the general public, this subchapter aims to inspire deeper reflection and dialogue on these profound and enduring questions.

Theistic Evolution: Harmonizing Science and Religion

In today's society, the debate between science and religion often seems like an unbridgeable chasm. However, many modern scientists are challenging this notion, proposing a perspective that seeks to harmonize these seemingly opposing forces. This subchapter explores the concept of theistic evolution – a view that aims to reconcile scientific understanding with religious beliefs.

Theistic evolution proposes that the principles of evolution, as understood by biologists, can coexist with the concept of a divine creator. Scientists who hold this perspective acknowledge the overwhelming evidence supporting the theory of evolution and accept that it provides a comprehensive explanation for the diversity of life on Earth. Simultaneously, they believe that this process of evolution is guided and overseen by a higher power.

Atheist scientists may find it difficult to accept theistic evolution since it challenges their rejection of any divine existence. However, theistic evolution offers a framework that allows them to explore the potential role of a higher power in the intricate workings of the universe, opening doors to new perspectives.

Agnostic scientists, on the other hand, see theistic evolution as a way to interpret the mysteries of life without committing to any specific religious doctrine. It offers them the opportunity to explore the possibility of a divine force while still maintaining a scientific mindset.

Theistic scientists, who already hold religious beliefs, find that theistic evolution provides a bridge between their faith and scientific understanding. They see the evidence of evolution as a testament to the complexity and beauty of God's creation, rather than a challenge to their religious beliefs.

Scientists in various fields contribute to this discourse from their unique perspectives. Evolutionary biologists examine the role of God in the creation of life, while physicists explore theories on the existence of a higher power or divine energy within the fundamental laws of the universe. Neuroscientists delve into the neurological basis of religious experiences and beliefs, shedding light on the connection between the brain and spirituality.

Environmental scientists and geneticists study God's relationship with nature and the genetic factors influencing religious beliefs and spirituality, respectively. Quantum physicists engage in discussions on the potential connection between God and the fundamental laws of the universe, while ethicists analyze the moral implications and ethical theories surrounding God's existence and influence on human behavior.

By exploring theistic evolution, scientists, theologians, and the public can find common ground, fostering a greater understanding between science and religion. This subchapter aims to provide a platform for the exchange of ideas and perspectives, encouraging dialogue and collaboration among these diverse fields. In doing so, it opens up new possibilities for a more holistic understanding of the mysteries of existence, where science and religion can coexist in harmony.

Evolutionary Biologists' Examination of God's Involvement in the Natural World

Evolutionary biology has long been at the forefront of scientific investigations into the origin and development of life on Earth. As scholars dedicated to unraveling the mysteries of life's diversity and complexity, evolutionary biologists have naturally grappled with the question of God's involvement in the natural world. In this subchapter, we explore the diverse perspectives of evolutionary biologists on this intriguing topic.

For many evolutionary biologists, the theory of evolution itself has provided a compelling explanation for the development of life without the need for divine intervention. They argue that the natural processes of mutation, selection, and adaptation can account for the incredible diversity of species observed today. From their perspective, the notion of God as a creator is unnecessary to explain the evolutionary history of life on Earth.

However, not all evolutionary biologists hold this strictly atheistic perspective. Some adopt an agnostic stance, acknowledging the limits of scientific inquiry and leaving room for the possibility of a higher power or divine energy. These individuals recognize the inherent complexity of the natural world and do not dismiss the idea that there may be forces at play beyond our current understanding.

On the other end of the spectrum, there are evolutionary biologists who hold theistic beliefs and see no conflict between their scientific work and their faith in God. They view the process of evolution as a mechanism employed by God to bring about the diversity of life. For these scientists, the study of evolution enhances their appreciation of God's creative power and the intricate design of the natural world.

Evolutionary biologists also delve into the ethical implications of their work in relation to God's involvement. They explore the moral dimensions of evolution, considering questions such as the origins of altruism, the nature of suffering, and the potential influence of natural selection on human behavior. These discussions aim to shed light on the relationship between God's existence and the moral framework governing human actions.

In conclusion, evolutionary biologists offer a range of perspectives when examining God's involvement in the natural world. From atheistic viewpoints that attribute the development of life solely to natural processes, to agnostic and theistic perspectives that leave room for the divine, these scientists contribute valuable insights to the ongoing dialogue between science and spirituality. By engaging in these discussions, scientists, theologians, and the public can foster a deeper understanding of the intricate relationship between the natural world and the divine.

Debates and Controversies Surrounding Evolution and God

In the ongoing dialogue between science and religion, one of the most contentious subjects is the relationship between evolution and the existence of God. This subchapter delves into the multifaceted debates and controversies that have emerged among scientists, theologians, and the public regarding this crucial topic.

Atheist scientists' perspective on God forms a significant part of this discourse. Many atheists contend that the theory of evolution, supported by overwhelming scientific evidence, obviates the need for a divine creator. They propose that the natural processes of mutation, adaptation, and natural selection can fully explain the complexity and diversity of life on Earth. These scientists argue that attributing the existence of life to a higher power is unnecessary and unscientific.

Conversely, agnostic scientists approach the topic with more uncertainty. They neither affirm nor deny the existence of God, recognizing the limitations of scientific knowledge in addressing metaphysical questions. Agnostic scientists explore different interpretations of God, acknowledging the possibility of a divine force while admitting that it remains beyond empirical understanding.

Theistic scientists, on the other hand, firmly believe in the existence of God and seek to reconcile their religious beliefs with scientific findings. They propose that evolution is a mechanism designed and guided by a higher intelligence, emphasizing the compatibility between faith and science. Theistic scientists argue that God's role in the creation of life can be understood through a deeper exploration of the natural world.

Evolutionary biologists play a crucial role in this debate, as they investigate the mechanisms and processes through which life has evolved. While many evolutionary biologists hold atheistic or agnostic views, some contend that God's influence is evident in the intricate patterns and complexity of the evolutionary process.

Physicists contribute to the discussion by exploring theories on the existence of a higher power or divine energy. Some physicists propose that the fundamental laws governing the universe reflect an underlying intelligent design, suggesting the existence of a cosmic creator.

Neuroscientists delve into the neurological basis of religious experiences and beliefs, examining the brain's role in shaping individual spirituality. They explore the question of whether religious experiences are solely a product of brain activity or if they offer a glimpse into a transcendent reality.

Environmental scientists provide unique perspectives on God's relationship with nature and the environment. They explore the ethical implications of ecological degradation and advocate for a renewed understanding of humanity's role as stewards of the Earth.

Geneticists investigate the genetic factors that influence religious beliefs and spirituality, aiming to uncover potential biological underpinnings. Their studies shed light on the complex interplay between genetics, environment, and belief systems.

Quantum physicists engage in discussions on the potential connection between God and the fundamental laws of the universe. They explore the mysterious nature of quantum mechanics and contemplate how it relates to the divine.

Finally, ethicists analyze the moral implications and ethical theories surrounding God's existence and influence on human behavior. They examine the impact of religious beliefs on societal norms, individual decision-making, and the pursuit of justice.

As the debates and controversies surrounding evolution and God continue to unfold, this subchapter offers a comprehensive overview of the diverse perspectives held by scientists, theologians, and the public. By engaging with these different viewpoints, we can foster a deeper understanding of the complex relationship between science, religion, and the mysteries of existence.

Chapter 6: Physicists' Theories on the Existence of a Higher Power or Divine Energy

Quantum Mechanics and its Philosophical Implications

Quantum mechanics, the branch of physics that deals with the behavior of matter and energy on the smallest scales, has revolutionized our understanding of the universe. Its principles, such as superposition and entanglement, have challenged long-held assumptions about reality and forced scientists and philosophers to grapple with profound questions about the nature of existence. In this subchapter, we will explore the philosophical implications of quantum mechanics and its relevance to our understanding of God.

For atheist scientists, the discoveries of quantum mechanics have provided further evidence against the existence of a higher power. The probabilistic nature of quantum phenomena suggests a universe governed by chance rather than divine design. They argue that the laws of physics, not the hand of a creator, can explain the complexity and diversity of the natural world.

Agnostic scientists take a more nuanced approach, recognizing the limitations of human knowledge. They acknowledge the profound mysteries revealed by quantum mechanics and remain open to the possibility of a higher power, while emphasizing the need for empirical evidence and scientific inquiry.

In contrast, theistic scientists find in quantum mechanics a deep resonance with their beliefs. They see the inherent order and fine-tuning in the fundamental laws of the universe as evidence of a guiding intelligence. They argue that quantum phenomena, with their potential for non-locality and interconnectedness, offer a glimpse into the divine nature.

Evolutionary biologists, on their part, explore the role of God in the creation of life. While some see evolution as a purely natural process, others propose that God's influence may be found in the underlying mechanisms that allow for the emergence of complexity and adaptation.

Physicists delve into the question of whether the fundamental laws of the universe point to a higher power or divine energy. Some propose that the very existence of these laws and their mathematical elegance suggest an underlying order that can be attributed to a transcendent source.

Neuroscientists study the neurological basis of religious experiences and beliefs. They seek to understand how the brain processes and interprets religious experiences, exploring the possibility that these experiences may have a natural basis but may also transcend the physical realm.

Environmental scientists examine God's relationship with nature and the environment. They explore the ethical implications of our stewardship of the Earth and the responsibility we have to preserve and protect the environment as a reflection of our reverence for the divine.

Geneticists investigate the genetic factors influencing religious beliefs and spirituality. They explore the interplay between genetics and personal religious experiences, seeking to understand the complex nature of faith and spirituality.

Quantum physicists engage in discussions on the potential connection between God and the fundamental laws of the universe. They explore the possibility that the mysterious phenomena of quantum mechanics may offer clues to the nature of God and the underlying fabric of reality.

Finally, ethicists analyze the moral implications and ethical theories surrounding God's existence and influence on human behavior. They grapple with questions of free will, moral responsibility, and the nature of good and evil in light of the belief in a higher power.

In conclusion, the philosophical implications of quantum mechanics are vast and varied. They challenge our preconceived notions, inspire awe and wonder, and provoke deep reflections on the nature of God and our place in the universe. The perspectives of scientists, theologians, and the public on these implications are diverse, reflecting the complexity of the subject matter and the deeply personal nature of our beliefs and understanding of the divine.

Physicists' Search for a Unified Theory of Everything

In the quest to understand the fundamental laws that govern the universe, physicists have long been intrigued by the possibility of a unified theory of everything. This subchapter explores the perspectives of scientists on the existence of a higher power or divine energy, and how it relates to their search for a unified theory.

For many atheist scientists, the idea of God is seen as a human construct, a product of our need for answers in the face of the unknown. They argue that science provides a rational explanation for the workings of the universe, eliminating the need for a divine entity.

On the other hand, agnostic scientists acknowledge the limitations of human knowledge and are open to the possibility of a higher power. They believe that science can only take us so far in understanding the universe, and there may be phenomena that lie beyond our current scientific understanding.

Theistic scientists, who believe in the existence of God, see their work as a way to uncover the divine plan and understand God's creation. They view the search for a unified theory as a means to unravel the intricacies of the universe and gain a deeper understanding of the divine.

In the realm of physics, evolutionary biologists explore the role of God in the creation of life. They seek to reconcile the concept of a higher power with the principles of evolution, examining how God's influence may have shaped the processes that led to the emergence of life on Earth.

Quantum physicists delve into the mysteries of the subatomic world, contemplating the potential connection between God and the fundamental laws of the universe. They explore the possibility that the underlying fabric of reality may hold clues to the existence of a higher power.

Neuroscientists, in their exploration of the neurological basis of religious experiences and beliefs, attempt to understand how the brain processes and interprets spirituality. They investigate whether such experiences are purely biological phenomena or if they have a connection to something beyond the physical realm.

Environmental scientists examine God's relationship with nature and the environment. They explore the idea of God as a steward of the Earth and the ethical implications of our responsibility towards the environment.

Geneticists study the genetic factors influencing religious beliefs and spirituality, seeking to understand if there are biological predispositions to faith. They investigate whether our genes play a role in shaping our perceptions of the divine.

Lastly, ethicists analyze the moral implications and ethical theories surrounding God's existence and influence on human behavior. They explore the impact of religious beliefs on our ethical frameworks and consider whether our understanding of morality is intrinsically tied to the idea of a higher power.

The search for a unified theory of everything has captivated the minds of physicists for centuries. As scientists, theologians, and the public continue to explore the various dimensions of God's existence and influence, the quest for understanding the divine equation that underlies the universe remains an ongoing endeavor.

The Concept of God in Quantum Physics

In recent years, the field of quantum physics has opened up fascinating new avenues of exploration into the nature of reality. As scientists delve deeper into the fundamental laws that govern the universe, intriguing questions arise regarding the existence of a higher power or divine energy. This subchapter aims to explore the concept of God within the framework of quantum physics, presenting diverse perspectives from scientists, theologians, and the public.

Atheist scientists often dismiss the idea of God as a mere human construct, arguing that the principles of quantum physics can account for the complexity and beauty of the universe without the need for a supernatural explanation. They emphasize that the laws of physics, such as quantum superposition and entanglement, can give rise to the emergence of life and consciousness.

On the other hand, agnostic scientists take a more open-minded approach, acknowledging the limits of human understanding and leaving room for the possibility of a higher power. They propose that quantum phenomena, such as wave-particle duality and the observer effect, hint at a deeper reality beyond our current comprehension, potentially pointing to the presence of God.

Theistic scientists, who hold strong religious beliefs, find harmony between their faith and the principles of quantum physics. They argue that the complex and finely-tuned nature of the universe, as revealed by quantum mechanics, can be seen as evidence of an intelligent designer. They perceive God as the creative force behind the laws of physics, setting the stage for the emergence of life and consciousness.

Evolutionary biologists provide interesting insights into the role of God in the creation of life. They propose that the process of evolution can be viewed as God's method of bringing forth diversity and complexity, with natural selection acting as a mechanism for adaptation and survival.

Physicists, deeply immersed in the study of quantum phenomena, offer various theories on the existence of a higher power or divine energy. Some speculate that consciousness itself may be a fundamental aspect of the universe, intimately connected to the underlying fabric of reality.

Neuroscientists explore the neurological basis of religious experiences and beliefs, seeking to understand the mechanisms by which individuals perceive and connect with the divine. They investigate how religious experiences can be explained through the activation of specific brain regions and the release of neurotransmitters.

Environmental scientists consider God's relationship with nature and the environment. They explore the idea that the intricate balance and interconnectedness observed in ecosystems could be seen as evidence of a divine presence, prompting discussions on the ethical responsibilities humans have towards the natural world.

Geneticists delve into the genetic factors influencing religious beliefs and spirituality. They investigate the role of specific genes and their interaction with environmental factors in shaping an individual's propensity for religious experiences and the development of their spiritual beliefs.

Quantum physicists engage in discussions on the potential connection between God and the fundamental laws of the universe. They explore the concept of a cosmic consciousness or divine energy that pervades all of existence, suggesting that the very fabric of reality is imbued with a higher intelligence.

Ethicists analyze the moral implications and ethical theories surrounding God's existence and influence on human behavior. They delve into questions of free will, moral responsibility, and the grounding of ethical principles in a divine source.

In conclusion, the concept of God in the realm of quantum physics is a topic that elicits diverse viewpoints from scientists, theologians, and the general public. This subchapter provides a platform for scientists and scholars from various fields to explore and discuss their perspectives on the potential connection between God and the fundamental laws of the universe. It aims to foster a deeper understanding and appreciation of the intricate relationship between science, spirituality, and the nature of existence.

Speculations and Hypotheses about a Divine Energy

In the quest to understand the mysteries of the universe, scientists and theologians alike have been intrigued by the concept of a divine energy. This subchapter delves into the various speculations and hypotheses put forth by experts from diverse fields, shedding light on the intriguing relationship between science and spirituality.

Atheist scientists, known for their skepticism towards the existence of God, provide valuable insights into the nature of a divine energy. They propose that the concept of God may be a metaphorical representation of the intricate laws and forces governing the universe. By exploring the laws of physics, they seek to unravel the fundamental principles that underpin the cosmos, ultimately leading to a better understanding of this divine energy.

On the other hand, agnostic scientists offer interpretations of a divine energy that acknowledge the limitations of human knowledge. They propose that while we may never fully comprehend the nature of God, it is possible to explore the different ways in which individuals experience and interpret this energy. By examining religious experiences and beliefs from a neurological perspective, neuroscientists contribute to this discussion, highlighting the potential role of the brain in shaping religious experiences.

Theistic scientists, who hold strong beliefs in God, provide their personal insights into the existence and understanding of a divine energy. They argue that scientific discoveries can coexist with religious faith, and that God may have influenced the creation and evolution of life. Evolutionary biologists, in particular, explore the role of God in the development of complex life forms, offering thought-provoking perspectives on the intersection of science and spirituality.

Physicists delve into the fundamental laws of the universe, proposing theories on the existence of a higher power or divine energy. They speculate about the potential connections between the laws of physics and the nature of God, raising questions about the origins and purpose of the universe.

Environmental scientists contribute to this discourse by examining God's relationship with nature and the environment. They explore the ethical implications of our treatment of the planet, considering whether our actions align with the concept of a divine energy that nurtures and sustains all living beings.

Geneticists, meanwhile, study the genetic factors that influence religious beliefs and spirituality. By investigating the biological basis of these experiences, they shed light on the potential interplay between our genes and our perception of a divine energy.

Quantum physicists explore the potential connection between God and the fundamental laws of the universe. They propose that the nature of reality itself may be influenced by a divine energy, with quantum mechanics providing a framework for understanding this complex relationship.

Ethicists analyze the moral implications and ethical theories surrounding God's existence and influence on human behavior. They explore how belief in a divine energy shapes our understanding of right and wrong, and how it influences our decision-making processes.

In this subchapter, scientists, theologians, and the public are invited to engage in an interdisciplinary exploration of the concept of a divine energy. By considering the perspectives of various scientific disciplines, we hope to foster a deeper understanding of the relationship between science, spirituality, and the mysteries of the universe.

Chapter 7: Neuroscientists' Exploration of the Neurological Basis of Religious Experiences and Beliefs

Neurological Explanations for Religious Experiences

In recent years, the field of neuroscience has made significant strides in unraveling the mysteries of the human brain. One area of particular interest is the study of religious experiences and beliefs, which were once solely the domain of theologians and philosophers. Neuroscientists have begun to explore the neurological basis of these experiences, shedding light on how the brain processes and interprets religious phenomena.

Religious experiences, such as feelings of transcendence, a sense of awe, or a connection to something greater than oneself, have long been considered deeply personal and spiritual in nature. However, recent research suggests that there may be underlying neurological mechanisms at play. Neuroscientists have found that certain areas of the brain, such as the prefrontal cortex and the limbic system, are consistently activated during religious experiences. These regions are associated with emotion, reward processing, and social cognition, providing insights into the brain's response to religious stimuli.

Furthermore, studies have shown that individuals who report more frequent and intense religious experiences tend to have greater neural connectivity in specific brain networks. These networks, known as the default mode network and the salience network, are involved in self-referential thinking, introspection, and the processing of emotional and social information. The heightened connectivity within these networks may contribute to the profound and transformative nature of religious experiences.

While these findings provide intriguing insights into the neurological basis of religious experiences, they do not discount the possibility of a spiritual dimension beyond the physical brain. Scientists, theologians, and the public alike must consider the multidimensional nature of human existence, where neurological processes may interact with metaphysical realities.

For scientists, these neurological explanations for religious experiences offer a new lens through which to understand the nature of belief and spirituality. For theologians, it opens up a dialogue between science and religion, where the findings of neuroscience can enrich and deepen our understanding of faith. And for the public, this research provides a bridge between the realms of science and spirituality, fostering a more holistic and integrated understanding of the human experience.

In conclusion, while the neurological explanations for religious experiences provide valuable insights into the workings of the brain, they do not diminish the profound and personal nature of spirituality. Rather, they invite us to embrace a more nuanced understanding of the human experience, where science and religion can coexist and inform one another. As we continue to explore the mysteries of the brain, we may come to appreciate the intricate interplay between the physical and the spiritual, and the divine equation that underlies our existence.

Investigating the Brain's Response to Religious Stimuli

Religion has long been a subject of fascination and debate, with people across the globe holding diverse beliefs and interpretations. In recent years, scientists from various fields have turned their attention to understanding the brain's response to religious stimuli, shedding light on the neural mechanisms underlying religious experiences and beliefs. This subchapter delves into the intriguing world of neuroscience and its exploration of the neurological basis of religious experiences and beliefs.

Neuroscientists have embarked on a groundbreaking journey to unravel the mysteries of the brain's response to religious stimuli. Through cutting-edge technologies such as functional magnetic resonance imaging (fMRI) and electroencephalography (EEG), they have been able to map the neural networks involved in religious experiences, prayer, meditation, and other spiritual practices.

Studies have shown that when individuals engage in religious activities, specific regions of the brain become activated. For example, the prefrontal cortex, associated with cognitive processing and decision-making, plays a crucial role in religious belief formation. The limbic system, involved in emotion and reward processing, also shows heightened activity during religious experiences.

Furthermore, neuroscientists have explored the role of neurotransmitters, such as dopamine and serotonin, in shaping religious experiences. These chemicals modulate emotions and play a vital part in feelings of transcendence, awe, and spiritual ecstasy.

However, it is important to note that the brain's response to religious stimuli is not limited to believers alone. Atheist and agnostic scientists have offered alternative explanations, suggesting that these experiences can be attributed to purely naturalistic processes. They argue that religious experiences may arise from the brain's innate capacity for generating altered states of consciousness, rather than being evidence of a divine presence.

The findings from neuroscience also have implications for the understanding of religious beliefs and spirituality. Geneticists have begun exploring the genetic factors that influence an individual's propensity for religious belief, shedding light on the complex interplay between biology and faith.

As scientists and theologians continue to engage in dialogue, it is becoming increasingly clear that the human brain plays a central role in shaping and influencing religious experiences and beliefs. The exploration of the neurological basis of religion provides a captivating avenue for bridging the gap between science and spirituality, offering new insights into the nature of human consciousness and the diverse ways in which individuals experience the divine.

In conclusion, the investigation of the brain's response to religious stimuli has opened up an exciting frontier of research. This subchapter has explored the findings of neuroscientists and their efforts to understand the neural mechanisms underlying religious experiences and beliefs. As scientists, theologians, and the public continue to delve into these fascinating discoveries, we can expect a deeper understanding of the complex relationship between the brain, religion, and human spirituality.

The Evolutionary Origins of Religious Beliefs

Religious beliefs have been a fundamental aspect of human existence throughout history, but what are the evolutionary origins of these beliefs? This subchapter explores the scientific perspectives on the development and significance of religious beliefs, delving into various disciplines to shed light on this intriguing subject.

Evolutionary biologists propose that religious beliefs may have emerged as a byproduct of cognitive processes that evolved for other purposes. Our ancestors' ability to detect agency, perceive patterns, and infer intentions allowed them to navigate their social and natural environment successfully. These cognitive tendencies might have predisposed humans to develop beliefs in supernatural beings or forces, as a way to make sense of the world and establish social cohesion.

Physicists offer different theories on the existence of a higher power or divine energy. Some argue that the laws of physics themselves are evidence of a grand design, while others suggest the possibility of multiple universes or dimensions that could accommodate a divine realm. These theories provoke thought and challenge traditional religious interpretations, encouraging a synthesis of scientific and spiritual perspectives.

Neuroscientists explore the neurological basis of religious experiences and beliefs. By studying the brain activity of individuals during prayer, meditation, or religious rituals, they aim to understand the neural mechanisms underlying these experiences. Their findings suggest that religious experiences involve specific brain regions, neurotransmitters, and neural networks, shedding light on the physiological basis of religious phenomena.

Environmental scientists provide valuable insights into the relationship between God and nature. They examine how religious beliefs shape attitudes towards the environment, conservation efforts, and sustainability. By integrating religious values and environmental ethics, they aim to foster a deeper understanding of humanity's responsibility towards the natural world.

Geneticists investigate the genetic factors influencing religious beliefs and spirituality. Through studies on twins and families, they explore the heritability of religious traits and seek to identify specific genes associated with religious experiences. These findings contribute to the ongoing nature versus nurture debate and provide a scientific perspective on the genetic basis of religious tendencies.

Quantum physicists engage in fascinating discussions on the potential connection between God and the fundamental laws of the universe. They explore the concept of a universal consciousness or cosmic intelligence that underlies the quantum realm, challenging traditional notions of a distant, separate deity.

Ethicists analyze the moral implications and ethical theories surrounding God's existence and influence on human behavior. They examine the role of religious beliefs in shaping moral values, ethical decision-making, and societal norms. By delving into various ethical frameworks, they contribute to the ongoing dialogue between science, religion, and ethics.

In conclusion, this subchapter provides a comprehensive exploration of the evolutionary origins of religious beliefs. By drawing upon the perspectives of evolutionary biologists, physicists, neuroscientists, environmental scientists, geneticists, quantum physicists, and ethicists, it offers a multidisciplinary approach to understanding the complex interplay between science and religion. Scientists, theologians, and the public alike will find valuable insights into the origins, nature, and significance of religious beliefs, fostering a deeper appreciation for the diversity of human experiences and beliefs.

Implications for the Understanding of God and Religion

In "The Divine Equation: Modern Scientists' Published Views About God," we delve into the multifaceted perspectives of scientists on the profound concepts of God and religion. This subchapter explores the implications of these perspectives, offering insights that bridge the gap between science and theology. Addressed to scientists, theologians, and the public, this chapter sheds light on the diverse range of opinions expressed by different scientific disciplines.

Atheist scientists' perspective on God challenges traditional religious beliefs by asserting the absence of a divine being. Their viewpoints encourage a critical examination of religious dogmas and promote discussions on secular ethics and morality. Conversely, agnostic scientists' interpretations of God acknowledge the limitations of human knowledge, recognizing the possibility of a higher power while emphasizing the importance of empirical evidence and rational inquiry.

Theistic scientists' beliefs and understanding of God offer a unique perspective, as they strive to reconcile their faith with scientific principles. Their exploration of God's existence and role in the universe fosters a dialogue between science and religion, encouraging a more nuanced understanding of both realms.

Evolutionary biologists' views on God's role in the creation of life explore the compatibility between evolution and religious beliefs. By examining the intricate processes that shape life on Earth, their research highlights the dynamic interplay between science and spirituality.

Physicists' theories on the existence of a higher power or divine energy probe the fundamental laws of the universe. Their investigations into the nature of reality challenge conventional notions, prompting reflection on the potential connection between God and the intricate fabric of the cosmos.

Neuroscientists' exploration of the neurological basis of religious experiences and beliefs offers valuable insights into the human mind's capacity for spirituality. By studying the brain mechanisms associated with religious encounters, they contribute to a deeper understanding of the origins and nature of religious experiences.

Environmental scientists' perspectives on God's relationship with nature and the environment emphasize the need for ecological stewardship. By examining the intrinsic value of nature and our responsibility towards it, they promote a more holistic understanding of God's presence in the world.

Geneticists' studies on the genetic factors influencing religious beliefs and spirituality shed light on the complex interplay between nature and nurture. Their research highlights the potential biological underpinnings of religious experiences, offering a new dimension to the understanding of human spirituality.

Quantum physicists' discussions on the potential connection between God and the fundamental laws of the universe challenge our conventional notions of reality. Their exploration of quantum phenomena raises questions about the nature of consciousness and its relation to the divine.

Ethicists' analysis of the moral implications and ethical theories surrounding God's existence and influence on human behavior invites critical reflection on the intersection of religion and ethics. By examining the moral frameworks shaped by religious beliefs, they contribute to the ongoing dialogue on the role of religion in guiding human behavior.

"The Divine Equation" aims to foster an inclusive dialogue, transcending the boundaries between science and religion. By exploring these various perspectives, we hope to inspire a deeper understanding of the implications of scientific thought on our understanding of God and religion. Through interdisciplinary conversations, we can forge new paths towards a more holistic perspective that encompasses both scientific inquiry and spiritual exploration.

Chapter 8: Environmental Scientists' Perspectives on God's Relationship with Nature and the Environment

The Concept of God in Relation to the Environment

In this subchapter, we delve into the intricate relationship between the concept of God and the environment. It is a topic that captures the attention and curiosity of scientists, theologians, and the public alike. The exploration of this subject is crucial as it brings together various perspectives, including those of modern scientists, atheist scientists, agnostic scientists, theistic scientists, evolutionary biologists, physicists, neuroscientists, environmental scientists, geneticists, quantum physicists, and ethicists.

Modern Scientists' Published Views About God:

Modern scientists have contributed significantly to the understanding of God by presenting their diverse perspectives. Their research and theories have shed light on the complex nature of the divine and its implications for our understanding of the environment.

Atheist Scientists' Perspective on God:

Atheist scientists offer thought-provoking arguments against the existence of God. Their views challenge traditional religious beliefs, prompting us to question the significance of God in relation to the environment.

Agnostic Scientists' Interpretations of God:

Agnostic scientists take a more nuanced approach, acknowledging the limits of human knowledge and the uncertainty surrounding the concept of God. Their interpretations provide a middle ground, inviting us to explore the mysteries of the divine with an open mind.

Theistic Scientists' Beliefs and Understanding of God:

Theistic scientists, on the other hand, hold firm to their beliefs in a higher power. Their scientific endeavors and spiritual convictions intertwine as they seek to understand God's role in the creation and sustenance of the environment.

Evolutionary Biologists' Views on God's Role in the Creation of Life:

Evolutionary biologists contribute fascinating insights into the interplay between God and the natural world. They explore the compatibility of evolution and religious beliefs, investigating the potential divine influence in the origins and development of life.

Physicists' Theories on the Existence of a Higher Power or Divine Energy:

Physicists offer unique perspectives on the existence of God, drawing upon theories such as the multiverse, string theory, and the anthropic principle. Their discussions provide a bridge between the mysteries of the universe and the concept of a higher power.

Neuroscientists' Exploration of the Neurological Basis of Religious Experiences and Beliefs:

Neuroscientists delve into the neural underpinnings of religious experiences and beliefs. By studying the brain, they aim to understand the relationship between the human mind, spirituality, and the concept of God.

Environmental Scientists' Perspectives on God's Relationship with Nature and the Environment:

Environmental scientists explore the interconnectedness of God, nature, and the environment. They analyze the moral and ethical implications of our treatment of the natural world, considering how our understanding of God influences our stewardship of the Earth.

Geneticists' Studies on the Genetic Factors Influencing Religious Beliefs and Spirituality:

Geneticists investigate the genetic factors that may influence religious beliefs and spirituality. By uncovering the biological basis of these phenomena, they contribute to our understanding of the complex interplay between genetics, God, and human behavior.

Quantum Physicists' Discussions on the Potential Connection Between God and the Fundamental Laws of the Universe:

Quantum physicists engage in thought-provoking discussions about the potential connection between God and the fundamental laws of the universe. They explore the profound implications of quantum mechanics for our understanding of the divine.

Ethicists' Analysis of the Moral Implications and Ethical Theories Surrounding God's Existence and Influence on Human Behavior:

Ethicists critically analyze the moral implications and ethical theories surrounding God's existence and influence on human behavior. They consider how our belief systems shape our ethical frameworks and guide our interactions with the environment.

This subchapter aims to present a comprehensive exploration of the concept of God in relation to the environment, drawing on the perspectives of scientists, theologians, and the wider public. By bringing together these diverse viewpoints, we hope to foster dialogue and encourage further research into this fascinating and complex topic.

Environmental Ethics and the Divine

In recent years, the intersection of environmental ethics and the concept of the divine has become a topic of great interest and debate among scientists, theologians, and the general public. The relationship between humanity's responsibility towards the environment and the existence or influence of a higher power has captivated the minds of thinkers from various disciplines.

For atheist scientists, the question of God's role in environmental ethics may seem irrelevant. However, their perspective on God is crucial to understanding the broader discourse. Atheist scientists often argue that environmental ethics should be grounded in secular values, such as the preservation of biodiversity, the prevention of pollution, and the sustainable use of resources. They believe that humanity has a moral obligation to protect the environment, irrespective of the divine.

On the other hand, agnostic scientists provide a more nuanced interpretation of God's relationship with nature and the environment. They acknowledge the possibility that a higher power exists but remain uncertain about its nature or influence. Agnostic scientists explore the ethical implications of various interpretations of God and how they may shape human behavior towards the environment.

Theistic scientists, who believe in the existence of a higher power, approach environmental ethics from a different perspective. They argue that the divine created the natural world and entrusted humans with its stewardship. Theistic scientists often find inspiration in religious texts that emphasize the importance of caring for the environment and view environmental degradation as a violation of divine will.

Moreover, evolutionary biologists delve into the potential role of God in the creation of life. They explore the compatibility between scientific theories of evolution and religious beliefs, examining the possibility of

God guiding the process of natural selection or establishing the initial conditions for life's emergence.

Physicists, neuroscientists, and geneticists contribute to the discourse by exploring the connection between God and the fundamental laws of the universe, the neurological basis of religious experiences and beliefs, and the genetic factors influencing religious beliefs and spirituality. Their research sheds light on the human perception of the divine, offering insights into how these perceptions may influence environmental attitudes and behaviors.

Environmental scientists also play a crucial role in this discussion, offering unique perspectives on God's relationship with nature and the environment. They explore how religious beliefs and spirituality can motivate individuals to take action in preserving the environment and advocate for sustainable practices.

Lastly, ethicists analyze the moral implications and ethical theories surrounding God's existence and influence on human behavior. They critically evaluate the ethical frameworks that stem from different interpretations of the divine and their implications for environmental ethics.

The subchapter "Environmental Ethics and the Divine" serves as a platform for scientists, theologians, and the public to engage in a multidisciplinary dialogue. By exploring the perspectives of diverse scientific disciplines and belief systems, it aims to foster a deeper understanding of the complex relationship between environmental ethics and the concept of the divine.

Sustainability and Stewardship in Religious Contexts

In the modern world, the concept of sustainability has become a crucial topic of discussion across various fields. From environmental science to ethics, sustainability is recognized as the key to securing a better future for our planet and all its inhabitants. However, it is often overlooked how religious contexts can play a vital role in promoting and practicing sustainability and stewardship.

Scientists, theologians, and the public are increasingly recognizing the significance of exploring the intersection between science and religion. The book "The Divine Equation: Modern Scientists' Published Views About God" delves into this dynamic relationship, presenting a diverse range of perspectives from atheist, agnostic, and theistic scientists, evolutionary biologists, physicists, neuroscientists, environmental scientists, geneticists, quantum physicists, and ethicists.

Within this wide array of scientific and theological viewpoints, the subchapter on "Sustainability and Stewardship in Religious Contexts" examines how different religious traditions and beliefs can inspire and guide sustainable practices. It explores how religious teachings and values can foster a sense of responsibility and stewardship towards the environment, as well as promote ethical behavior and sustainable lifestyles.

For example, environmental scientists contribute their perspectives on how various religious traditions view the relationship between God and nature. They discuss how these beliefs can influence attitudes towards environmental conservation and the responsible use of natural resources. Additionally, geneticists shed light on the genetic factors that may influence religious beliefs and spirituality, providing insights into the potential biological basis for our sense of connection to the natural world.

Furthermore, the subchapter delves into the ethical implications of God's existence and influence on human behavior. Ethicists analyze how religious beliefs and moral frameworks shape individuals' choices and actions, and how these can be harnessed to promote sustainable practices and environmental stewardship.

By exploring the intersection of sustainability and stewardship within religious contexts, this subchapter offers a comprehensive understanding of how religious beliefs and traditions can contribute to a more sustainable and environmentally conscious world. It invites scientists, theologians, and the public to engage in interdisciplinary dialogue and collaboration to address the pressing environmental challenges we face, bridging the gap between science and religion in pursuit of a better future for all.

Environmental Scientists' Role in Shaping Religious Environmentalism

Environmental scientists play a vital role in shaping religious environmentalism by providing scientific evidence and insights that challenge traditional religious beliefs and encourage a more harmonious relationship between humans and nature. This subchapter explores how environmental scientists contribute to the intersection of religion and environmentalism, addressing the concerns and perspectives of scientists, theologians, and the general public.

Environmental scientists provide evidence-based research on the impact of human activities on the environment, highlighting the urgent need for sustainable practices. Their work aims to bridge the gap between science and religion, offering a fresh perspective on how religious teachings can be interpreted in the context of environmental stewardship. By emphasizing the interconnectedness of all living beings and the Earth, environmental scientists encourage religious individuals to consider their responsibility in preserving the planet for future generations.

Moreover, environmental scientists challenge the anthropocentric view often associated with traditional religious beliefs, which prioritize human interests over the well-being of nature. They advocate for a more holistic understanding of God's relationship with the environment, emphasizing the inherent value and sacredness of all living beings. This perspective aligns with the teachings of many religious traditions that emphasize stewardship and compassion for the natural world.

Through their research, environmental scientists contribute to the development of ecotheology, a field that explores the spiritual dimensions of environmentalism. They provide theological frameworks that integrate scientific knowledge and religious beliefs, helping theologians and religious leaders develop a more nuanced understanding of God's presence in nature. This interdisciplinary approach fosters a sense of environmental responsibility grounded in both scientific evidence and religious teachings.

Additionally, environmental scientists' research on the impact of climate change and environmental degradation raises ethical questions about human behavior and societal values. They challenge individuals and communities to reflect on their role in the destruction of the planet, encouraging a reevaluation of consumerist lifestyles and unsustainable practices. By doing so, environmental scientists contribute to the broader conversation on the moral implications of God's existence and influence on human behavior.

In conclusion, environmental scientists play a crucial role in shaping religious environmentalism by providing scientific evidence, promoting a holistic understanding of God's relationship with nature, and contributing to the development of ecotheology. Their work encourages individuals and communities to reevaluate their attitudes towards the environment and embrace a more sustainable and compassionate approach to life. By bridging the gap between science and religion, environmental scientists foster a deeper understanding of God's presence in the natural world and inspire transformative action for the benefit of both humans and the planet.

Chapter 9: Geneticists' Studies on the Genetic Factors Influencing Religious Beliefs and Spirituality

Exploring the Genetic Basis of Religious Beliefs

In this subchapter, we delve into the fascinating field of genetics and its potential influence on religious beliefs and spirituality. While religious experiences and beliefs have traditionally been attributed to cultural, societal, and personal factors, recent research suggests that there may be a genetic component at play as well.

Geneticists have begun exploring the genetic factors that could influence an individual's religious beliefs and spirituality. Through the study of twins and family pedigrees, researchers have found evidence of a heritable component in religiousness. Studies have shown that identical twins, who share 100% of their genes, are more likely to have similar religious beliefs compared to fraternal twins, who share only 50% of their genes. These findings indicate that genetic factors may contribute to the development of religious beliefs.

But what specific genes are involved in shaping religious beliefs? Several candidate genes have been identified, such as the VMAT2 gene, which regulates the transport of neurotransmitters linked to feelings of well-being and happiness. Variations in this gene have been associated with differences in religiousness and spirituality.

However, it is important to note that genetics is not the sole determinant of religious beliefs. Environmental factors, personal experiences, and cultural influences also play significant roles. The interplay between genes and the environment is complex, and it is likely that both factors interact to shape an individual's religious inclinations.

This discussion also raises important questions about the implications of genetic influences on religious beliefs. For scientists, it opens up avenues for further research and understanding of the complex nature of human spirituality. Theologians may find it intriguing to explore how genetic factors can coexist with traditional religious teachings.

Furthermore, this exploration into the genetic basis of religious beliefs has implications for society as a whole. Understanding the genetic factors involved in religiousness could contribute to fostering tolerance and respect among different religious groups. It may also help individuals who struggle with their religious beliefs to better understand themselves and find acceptance.

In conclusion, the study of genetics has shed new light on the development of religious beliefs and spirituality. While genetics is not the sole determinant, it appears to play a role in shaping an individual's religious inclinations. This exploration prompts further interdisciplinary discussions among scientists, theologians, and the public, opening doors to better comprehend the complex nature of human spirituality and its relationship to genetics.

Genetic Predispositions and Spirituality

In the search for understanding the complex relationship between genetics and spirituality, scientists have been exploring the influence of genetic predispositions on religious beliefs and experiences. As we delve into this intriguing topic, it is crucial to acknowledge the diverse perspectives encompassed within the scientific and theological communities.

Atheist scientists, who reject the existence of a higher power, approach the study of genetic predispositions and spirituality from a different standpoint. They argue that religious experiences can be attributed to various neurological mechanisms rather than genetic factors. Agnostic scientists, on the other hand, maintain a more neutral stance, acknowledging the potential influence of genetic predispositions while remaining open to alternative explanations.

Theistic scientists, who firmly believe in the existence of God, seek to understand the genetic underpinnings of religious beliefs and spirituality to support their conviction. They propose that certain genetic variations may predispose individuals to be more inclined towards religious experiences, suggesting an evolutionary advantage to faith in a higher power.

Evolutionary biologists contribute to this discourse by exploring God's role in the creation of life. They consider the possibility that genetic factors may have shaped the development of religious beliefs as adaptive mechanisms, aiding in the survival and flourishing of human societies.

Physicists, known for their pursuit of understanding the fundamental laws of the universe, offer theories on the existence of a higher power or divine energy. They engage in discussions about the potential connections between God and the intricate fabric of reality, exploring the metaphysical implications of their scientific discoveries.

Neuroscientists, equipped with advanced tools for exploring the human brain, investigate the neurological basis of religious experiences and beliefs. Their studies focus on unraveling the intricate relationship between genetics, brain structure, and the formation of spiritual experiences, shedding light on the biological foundations of faith.

Environmental scientists, concerned with our relationship with the natural world, offer perspectives on God's connection with nature and the environment. They explore the moral and ethical implications of our stewardship of the Earth, contemplating the role of spirituality in motivating environmental actions.

Geneticists contribute valuable studies on the genetic factors influencing religious beliefs and spirituality. They investigate the heritability of faith, exploring how certain genetic variations may interact with environmental factors to shape an individual's religious inclinations.

Quantum physicists engage in thought-provoking discussions on the potential connection between God and the fundamental laws of the universe. They explore the possibility of a divine presence manifesting in the mysterious realms of quantum mechanics, challenging our understanding of reality and spirituality.

Ethicists add to this discourse by analyzing the moral implications and ethical theories surrounding God's existence and influence on human behavior. They explore the role of spirituality in shaping our moral compass and contemplate the implications of different religious beliefs on societal norms.

As we explore the interplay between genetics and spirituality, it is essential to approach this topic with an open mind, recognizing the complexity and diversity of perspectives within the scientific and theological communities. By embracing interdisciplinary dialogue, we can deepen our understanding of the profound and intricate relationship between genetics, spirituality, and our understanding of God.

Ethical Considerations in Genetic Research on Religion

Genetic research has revolutionized various fields of study, shedding light on the intricate mechanisms that shape human characteristics and behaviors. In recent years, scientists have begun exploring the genetic factors influencing religious beliefs and spirituality. This subchapter delves into the ethical considerations surrounding genetic research on religion, examining the implications for scientists, theologians, and the general public.

For scientists engaged in genetic research on religion, it is crucial to maintain the highest ethical standards. Respect for the autonomy and privacy of individuals must be paramount, ensuring that participation in such studies is voluntary and informed. Informed consent, comprehensive confidentiality measures, and protection of personal data are essential to safeguard the rights and well-being of research participants. Scientists should also engage in open dialogue with religious communities, seeking their input and addressing concerns to foster a collaborative and respectful approach.

Theologians and religious communities may have unique perspectives on genetic research and its implications for religious beliefs. It is important to engage in thoughtful dialogue and bridge the gap between scientific inquiry and religious teachings. The subchapter should encourage theologians and religious leaders to actively participate in the conversation, promoting an understanding that science and faith can coexist harmoniously.

The wider public, including atheists, agnostics, and theists, will undoubtedly have diverse opinions on genetic research on religion. Addressing concerns and misconceptions is crucial in fostering public trust and acceptance of such research. Clear communication about the goals, methods, and potential applications of genetic research on religion can help dispel fears and promote a sense of shared understanding.

Ethical considerations extend beyond the research itself and into the potential uses and applications of findings. The subchapter should explore the moral implications of genetic research on religion, emphasizing the importance of responsible and ethical interpretation of results. It should also address concerns related to potential stigmatization or discrimination based on genetic predispositions to certain religious beliefs or spiritual experiences.

In conclusion, genetic research on religion holds immense potential for deepening our understanding of the complex interplay between genetics and spirituality. However, it is vital to approach this research with utmost ethical considerations, ensuring respect for individual autonomy, privacy, and religious beliefs. By fostering collaboration and dialogue between scientists, theologians, and the public, we can navigate the ethical complexities and harness the benefits of genetic research on religion while promoting a harmonious coexistence between science and faith.

Implications for Understanding the Diversity of Religious Experiences

The study of the diversity of religious experiences holds profound implications for scientists, theologians, and the general public alike. By delving into the various perspectives of modern scientists on God, we gain invaluable insights into the multifaceted nature of religious belief and spirituality.

For atheist scientists, understanding the diversity of religious experiences allows for a deeper exploration of the human mind and the origins of belief systems. Their perspectives offer critical analyses of religious phenomena and challenge traditional notions of God, opening avenues for dialogue and intellectual growth.

Agnostic scientists, on the other hand, approach the diversity of religious experiences with curiosity and an open mind. They seek to interpret these experiences within the realm of scientific inquiry, acknowledging the existence of something beyond the material world while remaining uncertain about its nature.

Theistic scientists, who firmly believe in God's existence, find the study of religious experiences essential for deepening their understanding of the divine. By exploring the diverse ways in which individuals connect with the divine, they develop a rich tapestry of beliefs and practices that inform their own spiritual journeys.

Evolutionary biologists, in their exploration of God's role in the creation of life, delve into the intricacies of the natural world. They adopt a perspective that intertwines scientific understanding with religious belief, seeking to reconcile the processes of evolution with the existence of a higher power.

Physicists contribute to this discussion by presenting theories on the existence of a higher power or divine energy. By examining the fundamental laws of the universe, they explore the potential connections between God and the mysteries of the cosmos.

Neuroscientists offer a unique perspective, exploring the neurological basis of religious experiences and beliefs. Through their research, they shed light on the mechanisms that underlie spiritual encounters, providing a scientific lens through which to understand the profound impact of religion on the human brain.

Environmental scientists approach the diversity of religious experiences by examining God's relationship with nature and the environment. Their perspectives shed light on the ethical and moral implications of our treatment of the natural world, as well as the potential for religious beliefs to inspire environmental stewardship.

Geneticists contribute to this discourse by studying the genetic factors that influence religious beliefs and spirituality. Their research explores the intersection between nature and nurture, providing insights into the biological underpinnings of religious experiences.

Quantum physicists engage in discussions on the potential connection between God and the fundamental laws of the universe. Their exploration of the mysteries of quantum mechanics opens up possibilities for understanding the divine in a new light, challenging conventional notions of reality.

Finally, ethicists analyze the moral implications and ethical theories surrounding God's existence and influence on human behavior. By examining the impact of religious beliefs on individual and societal ethics, they contribute to a deeper understanding of the role of religion in shaping human values and behavior.

In conclusion, the implications of understanding the diversity of religious experiences are far-reaching and transcend disciplinary boundaries. By exploring the perspectives of modern scientists on God, we can enrich our understanding of spirituality, foster dialogue between science and religion, and cultivate a more inclusive and enlightened society.

Chapter 10: Quantum Physicists' Discussions on the Potential Connection between God and the Fundamental Laws of the Universe

Quantum Physics and the Nature of Reality

Quantum physics, the branch of science that explores the behavior of matter and energy at the smallest scales, has long fascinated scientists, theologians, and the public alike. Its findings, often perplexing and counterintuitive, have challenged our traditional notions of reality and opened up new possibilities for understanding the nature of the universe. In this subchapter, we delve into the intriguing world of quantum physics and its potential implications for our understanding of God and the divine.

For atheist scientists, quantum physics offers a unique perspective on the concept of God. They argue that the fundamental laws governing the universe can be explained purely through natural processes, without the need for a higher power. They view quantum phenomena, such as wave-particle duality and entanglement, as evidence that the universe operates according to purely physical principles.

Agnostic scientists, on the other hand, interpret quantum physics as a realm of uncertainty. They see the inherent unpredictability and indeterminism in quantum systems as a reflection of our limited knowledge and understanding. While they may not affirm or deny the existence of God, they acknowledge the possibility that there may be aspects of reality that lie beyond our current scientific grasp.

Theistic scientists, who believe in the existence of a higher power, find in quantum physics a source of wonder and awe. They see the intricate and finely tuned laws of quantum mechanics as evidence of an intelligent designer at work. They argue that the underlying order and complexity of the quantum world point to a purposeful creation.

Physicists, in their theories on the existence of a higher power or divine energy, explore the potential connections between quantum physics and spirituality. Some propose that consciousness itself may play a fundamental role in shaping reality, blurring the boundaries between the physical and the metaphysical.

Neuroscientists, studying the neurological basis of religious experiences and beliefs, seek to unravel the mechanisms behind our spiritual inclinations. They investigate how the brain processes and interprets religious experiences, shedding light on the neural underpinnings of faith.

Environmental scientists, meanwhile, offer perspectives on God's relationship with nature and the environment. They explore the ethical implications of our role as stewards of the Earth and consider how our understanding of the interconnectedness of all things, as revealed by quantum physics, can inform our environmental practices.

Geneticists, in their studies on the genetic factors influencing religious beliefs and spirituality, delve into the biological roots of our spiritual inclinations. They seek to uncover the genetic predispositions that may shape our beliefs and shed light on the evolutionary origins of faith.

Lastly, ethicists analyze the moral implications and ethical theories surrounding God's existence and influence on human behavior. They explore how our understanding of God and the divine can inform our moral decision-making and guide our actions in the world.

In this subchapter, we embark on a journey through the multifaceted world of quantum physics, examining its potential connections to God and the fundamental laws of the universe. Through the perspectives of scientists, theologians, and the general public, we aim to shed light on the intricate interplay between science, spirituality, and the nature of reality.

Quantum Entanglement and the Unity of All Things

In the exploration of the divine equation, one of the most fascinating phenomena that modern science has uncovered is quantum entanglement. This perplexing concept has captivated the minds of scientists, theologians, and the public alike, as it challenges our understanding of reality and hints at a deeper unity that connects all things.

Quantum entanglement refers to the strange and inexplicable phenomenon where two or more particles become linked in such a way that their states are instantly correlated, regardless of the distance between them. This means that the actions performed on one particle will instantaneously affect the other, defying our traditional notions of space and time. It is as if these particles, once entangled, share a mysterious connection that transcends the physical realm.

For scientists, this discovery has profound implications. Atheist scientists view quantum entanglement as a fundamental aspect of the natural world, explaining the interconnectedness of matter and energy without the need for a divine being. Agnostic scientists, on the other hand, interpret this phenomenon as a glimpse into a deeper reality, suggesting the possibility of a higher power or divine energy that orchestrates the interconnectedness of the universe.

Theistic scientists find solace in quantum entanglement as evidence of the divine plan. They see it as a reflection of God's omnipresence and omnipotence, illustrating that everything in the universe is intricately interconnected and guided by a higher intelligence. Evolutionary biologists, meanwhile, explore the role of God in the creation of life, contemplating how quantum entanglement might have influenced the emergence of complex organisms.

Physicists, ever in search of the ultimate truth, have put forth various theories on the existence of a higher power or divine energy. Some propose that quantum entanglement is the mechanism through which God manifests in the physical world, while others argue that it is the very fabric of God's existence itself.

Neuroscientists delve into the neurological basis of religious experiences and beliefs, examining how quantum entanglement might contribute to the profound sense of interconnectedness and spirituality that individuals often report. Environmental scientists ponder the relationship between God and nature, exploring how quantum entanglement might underpin the delicate balance of ecosystems.

Geneticists investigate the genetic factors influencing religious beliefs and spirituality, questioning whether quantum entanglement plays a role in shaping our predisposition towards faith. And quantum physicists engage in thought-provoking discussions on the potential connection between God and the fundamental laws of the universe, speculating on whether quantum entanglement is the bridge between the physical and the divine.

Ethicists, in turn, analyze the moral implications and ethical theories surrounding God's existence and influence on human behavior. They explore how quantum entanglement might not only shape the physical world but also impact our moral decision-making processes, as well as the implications this has for our understanding of free will and responsibility.

Quantum entanglement, with all its enigmatic qualities, serves as a focal point for scientists, theologians, and the public to contemplate the unity of all things. It invites us to consider the possibility that there is a deeper reality beyond what we can perceive, a reality that connects us all and hints at the existence of a divine presence. As we continue to unravel the mysteries of the universe, quantum entanglement serves as a constant reminder that there is still much we have yet to understand about the nature of existence and our place within it.

Quantum Cosmology and the Origin of the Universe

In the subchapter "Quantum Cosmology and the Origin of the Universe," we delve into the fascinating realm of quantum physics and its implications for understanding the origin of the universe. This chapter aims to provide insights and perspectives from a wide range of scientific disciplines, including physics, cosmology, and philosophy, to shed light on the nature of the universe and its potential connection to a higher power or divine energy.

For scientists, this subchapter presents an opportunity to explore the cutting-edge theories and research in quantum cosmology. It delves into the fundamental laws of the universe and how they may have given rise to the creation of the cosmos. From the perspective of atheist scientists, this discussion provides a platform to examine the possibility of a purely naturalistic explanation for the origin of the universe, challenging traditional religious narratives.

Agnostic scientists, on the other hand, can find in this subchapter a nuanced exploration of the limits of our current understanding. It delves into the philosophical implications of quantum cosmology and how it may shape our understanding of the concept of God. Theistic scientists, in turn, can explore the intersection between their religious beliefs and the scientific theories proposed by quantum physics.

Evolutionary biologists can also find relevance in this subchapter as it delves into their views on God's role in the creation of life. It explores the potential implications of quantum cosmology for understanding the emergence and development of life on Earth.

Physicists' theories on the existence of a higher power or divine energy are also examined, allowing for a deeper understanding of the various perspectives within the scientific community. Neuroscientists, in turn, can explore the neurological basis of religious experiences and beliefs, shedding light on the potential mechanisms by which individuals perceive and interact with the divine.

Environmental scientists can find relevance in this subchapter as it explores God's relationship with nature and the environment. It delves into the ethical implications of our understanding of God's existence and influence on human behavior, providing a platform for ethical analysis and debate among ethicists.

Lastly, geneticists can explore their studies on the genetic factors influencing religious beliefs and spirituality, contemplating the potential genetic basis for our understanding of God.

Together, this subchapter serves as a multidisciplinary exploration of quantum cosmology and the origin of the universe, providing a platform for scientists, theologians, and the public to engage in a thought-provoking dialogue about the fundamental questions of existence and the potential connection between science and spirituality.

Speculative Theories on God's Interaction with Quantum Reality

As we delve into the intricate and captivating world of quantum reality, a question arises: what is the role of God in this mysterious realm? In this subchapter, we will explore various speculative theories put forth by modern scientists, addressing the interaction between God and quantum reality.

Atheist scientists, known for their skepticism towards the existence of God, offer intriguing perspectives. Some propose that the seemingly random and probabilistic nature of quantum events could be evidence against the presence of an intelligent creator. They argue that if God existed, why would the fundamental laws of the universe rely on chance rather than deliberate design?

On the other hand, agnostic scientists take a more neutral stance, interpreting quantum reality as a potential gateway to understanding the nature of God. They suggest that the uncertainty and indeterminacy at the quantum level could be the result of God's intentional choice to allow free will and spontaneity within the universe.

Theistic scientists, who already believe in the existence of God, offer diverse explanations for God's interaction with quantum reality. Some propose that God guides the outcomes of quantum events, subtly influencing the course of the universe. Others suggest that God set the initial conditions of the universe in such a way that quantum phenomena naturally unfold according to a divine plan.

In the realm of evolutionary biology, scientists ponder God's role in the creation of life. Some argue that the emergence of life through natural processes is evidence of a divine guiding force, while others propose that God's influence lies in the initial creation and design of the laws that govern evolution itself.

Physicists, fascinated by the fundamental laws of the universe, explore the existence of a higher power or divine energy. They propose that the intricate mathematical equations governing quantum reality may be a glimpse into the mind of God, suggesting an underlying order and purpose that transcends our current understanding.

Neuroscientists delve into the neurological basis of religious experiences and beliefs, seeking to unravel the connection between the brain and the divine. They investigate whether religious experiences are simply the result of neural activity or if they offer a deeper connection to a higher power.

Environmental scientists contemplate God's relationship with nature and the environment. They explore the idea that the complexity and interconnectedness of ecosystems may reflect a divine plan, urging us to embrace a more respectful and sustainable approach to safeguarding the environment.

Meanwhile, geneticists study the genetic factors influencing religious beliefs and spirituality. They aim to uncover whether certain genetic predispositions play a role in shaping our perceptions and experiences of God.

Quantum physicists engage in discussions about the potential connection between God and the fundamental laws of the universe. They theorize that the very fabric of reality may be imbued with a divine presence, manifesting as the mysterious quantum phenomena that defy our classical understanding.

Lastly, ethicists analyze the moral implications and ethical theories surrounding God's existence and influence on human behavior. They explore how belief in God can shape our values, guide our actions, and contribute to the development of ethical frameworks.

In this subchapter, we have embarked on a journey through the minds of scientists, theologians, and the public, exploring their diverse perspectives on God's interaction with quantum reality. While these theories may remain speculative, they deepen our understanding of the complex relationship between science, faith, and the mysteries of the universe.

Chapter 11: Ethicists' Analysis of the Moral Implications and Ethical Theories Surrounding God's Existence and Influence on Human Behavior

Ethical Theories and the Divine Command Theory

In the realm of ethics, numerous theories have emerged to help us navigate the complexities of human behavior and moral decision-making. One such theory, the Divine Command Theory, posits that moral obligations are derived directly from a divine source.

The Divine Command Theory asserts that what is morally right or wrong is determined by God's commands. This theory suggests that God is the ultimate authority, and His commands serve as the foundation for ethical behavior. The theory holds that moral principles are not based on reason or human intuition but on the will of God. This perspective has been influential in shaping religious and philosophical discussions on morality throughout history.

For scientists and theologians, exploring the Divine Command Theory can shed light on the relationship between ethical principles and religious beliefs. Atheist scientists may approach this theory critically, questioning the existence of a divine source and arguing for alternative ethical frameworks based on reason and empathy.

Agnostic scientists, on the other hand, may interpret the Divine Command Theory as one of many possible explanations for moral obligations, recognizing that it is ultimately a matter of personal belief and faith.

Theistic scientists, who believe in a higher power, may find the Divine Command Theory aligns with their understanding of God's influence on human behavior and moral choices. They may argue that following God's commands leads to a more virtuous and fulfilling life.

Other scientific disciplines also offer unique perspectives on the Divine Command Theory. Evolutionary biologists may explore God's role, if any, in the creation of life, examining the compatibility between religious beliefs and scientific explanations of the origin of species.

Physicists may delve into theories on the existence of a higher power or divine energy, examining whether the fundamental laws of the universe point towards a divine creator. Neuroscientists may explore the neurological basis of religious experiences and beliefs, seeking to understand the mechanisms behind our perceptions of the divine.

Environmental scientists may examine God's relationship with nature and the environment, exploring the implications of religious teachings on environmental stewardship. Geneticists may study the genetic factors influencing religious beliefs and spirituality, investigating whether there are biological predispositions towards certain religious experiences.

Quantum physicists may engage in discussions on the potential connection between God and the fundamental laws of the universe, exploring the existence of a divine presence in the fabric of reality.

Finally, ethicists may analyze the moral implications and ethical theories surrounding God's existence and influence on human behavior. They may question whether the Divine Command Theory can provide a solid foundation for moral guidance or if other ethical frameworks are more applicable in a secular society.

In conclusion, the study of ethical theories, particularly the Divine Command Theory, offers scientists, theologians, and the public a rich framework for exploring the relationship between ethics and religious beliefs. By engaging in interdisciplinary discussions, we can gain a deeper understanding of morality, the nature of God, and how these concepts intersect with various scientific disciplines.

Moral Arguments for and against God's Existence

In "The Divine Equation: Modern Scientists' Published Views About God," we explore the multifaceted perspectives of scientists, theologians, and the general public on the existence of God. This subchapter delves into the moral arguments surrounding God's existence, shedding light on the ethical implications and theories that arise from these discussions.

For atheist scientists, God's existence is often seen as incompatible with their worldview. They argue that morality can be explained through evolutionary processes and societal norms rather than divine commandments. Their perspective challenges traditional religious beliefs and asserts that moral behavior can be understood through a secular lens.

On the other hand, theistic scientists firmly believe in a higher power and view God as the ultimate source of morality. They argue that objective moral values and duties can only exist if there is a divine being who establishes and upholds them. These scientists find solace in the notion that God's existence provides a foundation for ethical principles and guides human behavior.

Agnostic scientists take a more neutral stance, acknowledging the possibility of God's existence but remaining uncertain. They explore various interpretations of God, ranging from a deistic perspective where God is seen as a distant creator, to a pantheistic worldview where God is equated with the universe itself. These interpretations influence their understanding of morality and the role God plays in shaping human behavior.

Evolutionary biologists contribute to the discussion by exploring God's role in the creation of life. Some argue that the process of evolution itself is evidence against the existence of a divine creator, as it suggests that life has evolved through natural selection and random mutations rather than a deliberate act of creation. Others propose that God could have initiated and guided the evolutionary process, allowing for the coexistence of science and faith.

Physicists delve into theories on the existence of a higher power or divine energy. Some argue that the intricate laws of the universe point towards an intelligent designer, while others propose alternative explanations such as a multiverse or the laws of physics being self-sustaining. These theories provide diverse perspectives on the potential connection between God and the fundamental laws governing our universe.

Neuroscientists explore the neurological basis of religious experiences and beliefs. They investigate the brain mechanisms that underlie spiritual encounters, seeking to understand whether these experiences are purely physiological or if they offer evidence for the presence of a divine being. Their findings contribute to the ongoing dialogue between science and religion.

Environmental scientists offer their perspectives on God's relationship with nature and the environment. They debate whether God is the steward of the Earth, and if so, what implications this has for our responsibility towards the planet. These discussions highlight the importance of considering ethical and moral principles in our treatment of the environment.

Geneticists study the genetic factors influencing religious beliefs and spirituality. By exploring the genetic basis of faith, they shed light on the complex interplay between biology and religion, further deepening the understanding of human spirituality and its connection to God.

Quantum physicists engage in discussions on the potential connection between God and the fundamental laws of the universe. They explore the mysteries of quantum mechanics and contemplate whether these phenomena provide evidence for a higher power or divine energy. These debates contribute to the exploration of the fundamental nature of reality and our place within it.

Ethicists analyze the moral implications and ethical theories surrounding God's existence and influence on human behavior. They delve into questions of divine command ethics, moral absolutism, and moral relativism, seeking to understand how God's existence shapes our understanding of right and wrong.

"The Divine Equation: Modern Scientists' Published Views About God" offers a comprehensive exploration of the moral arguments for and against God's existence. By examining the perspectives of scientists, theologians, and the public, we hope to foster a deeper understanding of the complex relationship between science, morality, and faith.

Free Will and Moral Responsibility in Religious Contexts

In the realm of religious contexts, the concepts of free will and moral responsibility have long been subjects of intense debate and contemplation. Scientists, theologians, and the general public all have a vested interest in understanding how these concepts intersect with their beliefs about God and the nature of existence. This subchapter will delve into the various perspectives of scientists from different disciplines, shedding light on the multifaceted nature of this complex topic.

Atheist scientists often approach the question of free will and moral responsibility from a deterministic standpoint. They argue that the absence of a higher power negates the possibility of true free will, asserting that our actions are predetermined by the laws of nature and are thus not morally accountable. They question the existence of an objective moral framework, suggesting that moral responsibility is a societal construct.

Agnostic scientists, on the other hand, adopt a more contemplative approach. They acknowledge the limitations of human understanding and the inherent uncertainty surrounding the existence of God. While they may not subscribe to a particular religious doctrine, they recognize the potential for free will and moral responsibility as fundamental aspects of human experience, regardless of the source.

Theistic scientists, who believe in a higher power, often view free will and moral responsibility as integral components of their religious beliefs. They argue that God has endowed humans with the ability to make choices and be accountable for their actions. They see moral responsibility as a divine mandate, guided by religious teachings and divine commandments.

Evolutionary biologists contribute to the discussion by exploring God's role in the creation of life. They investigate the evolutionary origins of human behavior, seeking to understand how free will and moral responsibility have been shaped by natural selection. Some propose that our moral instincts have evolved to enhance cooperation and communal living.

Physicists, with their theories on the existence of a higher power or divine energy, offer unique perspectives on free will and moral responsibility. They contemplate the possibility of a cosmic consciousness or an underlying order that governs the universe, influencing human choices and actions.

Neuroscientists delve into the neurological basis of religious experiences and beliefs, investigating the brain's role in shaping our understanding of free will and moral responsibility. They explore the neural mechanisms underlying moral decision-making and the potential influence of religious experiences on ethical behavior.

Environmental scientists examine God's relationship with nature and the environment, considering the moral responsibility humans have towards the Earth and its resources. They explore the ethical implications of environmental degradation and advocate for sustainable practices based on their interpretation of religious teachings.

Geneticists study the genetic factors influencing religious beliefs and spirituality, seeking to unravel the complex interplay between biology and faith. They investigate the extent to which genetics may influence an individual's capacity for moral responsibility and the choices they make.

Quantum physicists engage in discussions on the potential connection between God and the fundamental laws of the universe. They explore the possibility of a deeper reality beyond our current understanding, where free will and moral responsibility may find their roots.

Ethicists analyze the moral implications and ethical theories surrounding God's existence and influence on human behavior. They critically examine the relationship between religious doctrines, free will, and moral responsibility, seeking to reconcile conflicting views and provide a framework for ethical decision-making.

In conclusion, the subchapter "Free Will and Moral Responsibility in Religious Contexts" explores the diverse perspectives of scientists, theologians, and the public on these profound philosophical questions. It offers a comprehensive understanding of how different disciplines contribute to our understanding of free will, moral responsibility, and their implications within religious frameworks.

Ethical Implications of Different Beliefs about God

In the realm of science and theology, the concept of God has been a subject of intense debate, exploration, and speculation. Scientists, theologians, and the public have presented a wide range of beliefs and interpretations about God, each with its own ethical implications. This subchapter delves into the ethical considerations arising from different perspectives on God, shedding light on the complex interplay between faith, reason, and morality.

Atheist scientists, who reject the existence of God, argue that ethical frameworks can be constructed without the need for divine authority. They contend that morality is a product of human reason, empathy, and societal values. Their perspective challenges traditional religious notions of morality and raises questions about the source and objectivity of ethical principles.

Agnostic scientists, on the other hand, adopt a more cautious stance, acknowledging the limitations of human knowledge in understanding God. Their interpretations of God emphasize a sense of uncertainty and open-mindedness, highlighting the importance of humility and tolerance in ethical decision-making.

Theistic scientists believe in the existence of a higher power and view God as the ultimate source of morality. They argue that ethical principles are grounded in divine revelation and that living in accordance with God's will leads to a virtuous life. Theistic perspectives offer a firm foundation for moral values but also raise challenges regarding the interpretation of religious texts and the potential for dogmatism.

Evolutionary biologists explore the role of God in the creation of life, investigating whether the processes of evolution are compatible with divine creation. Their views on God's involvement in natural selection and genetic variation have implications for how we perceive our place in the natural world and our moral responsibilities towards other living beings.

Physicists delve into theories on the existence of a higher power or divine energy, examining the fundamental laws of the universe. Their discussions on cosmology, quantum physics, and the origins of the universe shed light on the limits of human understanding and provoke ethical reflection on the awe-inspiring nature of the cosmos.

Neuroscientists explore the neurological basis of religious experiences and beliefs, examining the brain mechanisms underlying faith. Their studies provide insights into the psychological and physiological aspects of religious experiences, raising questions about the nature of spirituality and the potential for manipulation or exploitation of these experiences.

Environmental scientists examine God's relationship with nature and the environment, exploring the ethical implications of our stewardship or exploitation of the natural world. Their perspectives on the interconnectedness of all living beings and the responsibility we have towards future generations contribute to the discourse on sustainable development and environmental ethics.

Geneticists investigate the genetic factors influencing religious beliefs and spirituality, shedding light on the complex interplay between nature and nurture in shaping our worldview. Understanding the genetic basis of religious beliefs may inform discussions on free will, personal responsibility, and the potential for discrimination based on genetic predispositions.

Quantum physicists engage in discussions on the potential connection between God and the fundamental laws of the universe. Their explorations of the mysterious nature of reality and the interplay between consciousness and the physical world contribute to philosophical debates on the nature of God and our place in the cosmos.

Ethicists analyze the moral implications and ethical theories surrounding God's existence and influence on human behavior. They critically examine the diverse perspectives on God, evaluating their impact on moral decision-making, social cohesion, and the pursuit of justice and human flourishing.

In conclusion, the ethical implications of different beliefs about God are vast and multifaceted. The perspectives of scientists from various disciplines offer unique insights into the complex relationship between faith, reason, and morality. By engaging in open dialogue and respectful discourse, scientists, theologians, and the public can deepen their understanding of the ethical dimensions of different beliefs about God and foster a more inclusive and compassionate society.

Chapter 12: Conclusion

Summary of Findings

In "The Divine Equation: Modern Scientists' Published Views About God," we delve into the diverse perspectives of scientists on the topic of God. This subchapter aims to provide a comprehensive summary of the key findings from various scientific disciplines, as well as the implications for theology and the general public.

Starting with atheist scientists, their perspective on God is rooted in a disbelief in any supernatural entity. Through rigorous scientific inquiry, they argue that natural explanations can account for the phenomena traditionally attributed to God. Their skepticism challenges traditional religious beliefs and encourages critical thinking regarding the existence of a higher power.

Agnostic scientists, on the other hand, adopt a more neutral stance. They acknowledge the limitations of human knowledge and assert that the existence of God cannot be definitively proven or disproven. Their interpretations of God range from an abstract concept to an entity beyond human comprehension, leaving room for personal beliefs and interpretations.

Theistic scientists, who believe in the existence of God, offer a different perspective. They argue that the complexity and order observed in the universe provide evidence for a divine creator. Their beliefs and understanding of God vary across different religious traditions, shaping their scientific endeavors and influencing their worldview.

Evolutionary biologists explore the role of God in the creation of life. While some argue that evolutionary processes can coexist with religious beliefs, others see evolution as evidence of a purposeful design by a higher power. The interplay between science and religion in this field sparks philosophical debates about the nature of life and its origins.

Physicists delve into theories surrounding the existence of a higher power or divine energy. Some propose cosmological arguments that suggest the need for a creator to explain the fundamental laws and constants of the universe. Others explore the concept of a multiverse or parallel dimensions, seeking to understand the potential existence of a divine presence beyond our current understanding.

Neuroscientists delve into the neurological basis of religious experiences and beliefs. Through studying brain activity during moments of religious significance, they aim to unravel the cognitive processes underlying spirituality. Their work sheds light on the human capacity for religious experiences and offers insights into the nature of belief.

Environmental scientists examine God's relationship with nature and the environment. Some argue for a stewardship approach, emphasizing the responsibility of humans to care for the Earth as a divine gift. Others explore the presence of sacredness in nature, highlighting the spiritual connection between humans and the natural world.

Geneticists investigate the genetic factors that influence religious beliefs and spirituality. By examining the interplay between genetics and religion, they aim to understand the biological basis of faith. Their research contributes to the ongoing nature versus nurture debate within the context of religious experiences.

Quantum physicists engage in discussions about the potential connection between God and the fundamental laws of the universe. They explore the mysterious nature of quantum mechanics and its implications for the existence of a higher power. These discussions bridge the gap between science and metaphysics, inviting contemplation on the nature of reality.

Ethicists analyze the moral implications and ethical theories surrounding God's existence and influence on human behavior. They explore how religious beliefs shape ethical frameworks and guide human conduct. Their studies contribute to the ongoing dialogue on the intersection of faith, reason, and moral values.

This subchapter provides a glimpse into the multifaceted perspectives of scientists on God. It highlights the richness of the scientific discourse surrounding religion and encourages further exploration and dialogue among scientists, theologians, and the public. By fostering an interdisciplinary approach, we hope to bridge gaps, challenge assumptions, and deepen our collective understanding of the divine equation.

Implications for Science, Religion, and Society

In this subchapter, "Implications for Science, Religion, and Society," we delve into the profound impact that modern scientists' published views about God have on various aspects of our lives. This section aims to engage scientists, theologians, and the public alike, as we explore the diverse perspectives and interpretations surrounding God's existence and influence.

From the perspective of atheist scientists, we delve into their compelling arguments against the existence of God. These scientists challenge traditional religious beliefs, offering alternative explanations for the origins of life and the universe. We explore their reasoning, examining the implications of their views for science, religion, and society at large.

On the other hand, agnostic scientists offer a more nuanced perspective. They explore the limitations of human knowledge and the challenges in definitively proving or disproving the existence of God. We delve into their interpretations of God, which often focus on the mystery and uncertainty surrounding religious experiences.

Theistic scientists, who believe in God, provide their own unique insights. We explore their beliefs and understanding of God, examining how they reconcile their faith with scientific inquiry. These scientists shed light on the compatibility of science and religion, challenging the notion of an inherent conflict between the two.

We then turn to evolutionary biologists, who explore God's role in the creation of life. Through their research, we gain a deeper understanding of how religious beliefs and the theory of evolution can coexist. We examine the implications of their findings for religious interpretations of creation and the broader societal implications of these perspectives.

Physicists, in their theories on the existence of a higher power or divine energy, offer intriguing possibilities. We explore the potential connections between physics and spirituality, delving into the fundamental laws of the universe and their implications for understanding God.

Neuroscientists, in their exploration of the neurological basis of religious experiences and beliefs, shed light on the interplay between the brain and spirituality. We examine the implications of their research for understanding the nature of religious experiences and the role of the brain in shaping our beliefs.

Environmental scientists offer their perspectives on God's relationship with nature and the environment. We explore how this understanding can inform our approach to environmental conservation, sustainable practices, and our responsibility towards the natural world.

Geneticists, through their studies on the genetic factors influencing religious beliefs and spirituality, provide insights into the biological basis of faith. We explore the implications of these findings for understanding the diversity of religious experiences and beliefs within society.

Quantum physicists engage in discussions on the potential connection between God and the fundamental laws of the universe. We explore their theories, which challenge our understanding of reality and open up new possibilities for exploring the nature of God.

Finally, ethicists analyze the moral implications and ethical theories surrounding God's existence and influence on human behavior. We examine the impact of religious beliefs on societal values, ethical systems, and our understanding of right and wrong.

Through an exploration of these diverse perspectives, "Implications for Science, Religion, and Society" offers a comprehensive understanding of the complex relationship between science, religion, and society. By addressing the interests of scientists, theologians, and the public, this subchapter aims to foster dialogue and promote a deeper understanding of the implications of modern scientists' published views about God.

Future Directions for Research

As scientists, theologians, and the general public continue to explore the complex relationship between science and God, there are several intriguing avenues for future research that can shed light on the diverse perspectives on God's existence and influence. This subchapter delves into the potential future directions for research in various scientific disciplines, offering a glimpse into the exciting possibilities that lie ahead.

One promising area for exploration is the role of genetic factors in religious beliefs and spirituality. Geneticists can delve deeper into the genetic basis of religious inclinations, investigating whether there are specific genes that influence an individual's propensity to believe in God or engage in spiritual practices. This research can provide valuable insights into the biological underpinnings of religious experiences and help bridge the gap between science and faith.

Building on this biological aspect, neuroscientists can continue to explore the neurological basis of religious experiences and beliefs. By using advanced imaging techniques, researchers can uncover the brain regions involved in religious experiences and determine whether these experiences are unique or share common neural pathways with other emotional or transcendent experiences. This line of research holds the potential to deepen our understanding of the human brain's capacity for spiritual experiences.

In the realm of physics and cosmology, physicists can delve into theories on the existence of a higher power or divine energy. Exploring the fundamental laws of the universe and the origin of the cosmos, physicists can investigate whether there are inherent patterns or structures that suggest the presence of a guiding force. These studies can contribute to the ongoing dialogue between science and theology, offering new insights into the age-old question of God's existence.

Environmental scientists can also contribute to this dialogue by examining God's relationship with nature and the environment. By studying the intricate interconnections between ecosystems and the Earth's natural processes, researchers can gain a deeper understanding of how these systems reflect divine design or purpose. This research can foster a greater appreciation for the environment and potentially inform ethical considerations related to environmental stewardship.

Finally, ethicists can analyze the moral implications and ethical theories surrounding God's existence and influence on human behavior. By evaluating the impact of religious beliefs on individual and societal ethics, ethicists can provide valuable insights into the intersection of morality, religion, and science.

The future of research in the field of Modern Scientists' Published Views About God is rich and diverse. By embracing interdisciplinary collaborations and utilizing cutting-edge methodologies, scientists, theologians, and the public can continue to unravel the mysteries surrounding God's existence, influence, and humanity's relationship with the divine.

Closing Thoughts and Reflections

As we come to the end of our journey through the diverse and fascinating perspectives of scientists on the topic of God, it is important to take a moment for closing thoughts and reflections. Throughout the pages of this book, we have explored the intricate tapestry of ideas, theories, and beliefs that scientists from various disciplines have put forth regarding the existence and nature of God. From evolutionary biologists to quantum physicists, from neuroscientists to ethicists, each field has shed light on different aspects of this age-old question.

For scientists, theologians, and the general public alike, this compilation of modern scientists' published views about God has served as a bridge between the realms of science and spirituality. It has shown us that these seemingly opposing domains can coexist and even complement each other in our quest for knowledge and understanding.

One of the most striking aspects of this exploration has been the wide range of perspectives. Atheist scientists have shared their perspective, offering a critical examination of religious beliefs and the concept of God. Agnostic scientists have presented their interpretations, acknowledging the limits of human knowledge while remaining open to the possibility of a higher power. Theistic scientists have shared their deeply held beliefs and understanding of God, finding harmony between their faith and their scientific pursuits.

Evolutionary biologists have delved into the role of God in the creation of life, offering insights into the natural processes that have shaped our world. Physicists have presented theories on the existence of a higher power or divine energy, exploring the fundamental laws of the universe. Neuroscientists have embarked on an exploration of the neurological basis of religious experiences and beliefs, shedding light on the complex interplay between the brain and spirituality.

Environmental scientists have shared their perspectives on God's relationship with nature and the environment, highlighting the importance of stewardship and a sense of awe and wonder. Geneticists have contributed studies on the genetic factors influencing religious beliefs and spirituality, uncovering the intricate connections between our biology and our spiritual inclinations. Quantum physicists have engaged in discussions on the potential connection between God and the fundamental laws of the universe, pushing the boundaries of our understanding.

Finally, ethicists have analyzed the moral implications and ethical theories surrounding God's existence and influence on human behavior, offering valuable insights into the intersection of faith and morality.

In closing, "The Divine Equation: Modern Scientists' Published Views About God" has provided a platform for dialogue, understanding, and appreciation of the multifaceted nature of the question of God. It is through these diverse perspectives that we can continue to explore, question, and expand our understanding of the universe and our place within it. May this book serve as a catalyst for further exploration, collaboration, and the bridging of gaps between science, theology, and the public.

www.ingramcontent.com/pod-product-compliance
Lightning Source LLC
Chambersburg PA
CBHW051903130726

47987CB00002B/956